Advanced Wiccan Spirituality

Volume 1:
Revitalising the Roots and Foundations

Kevin Saunders

Green Magic

This edition is published by

Green Magic
Long Barn
Sutton Mallet
TA7 9AR
England

Typeset by Academic + Technical, Bristol
Printed and bound by Antony Rowe Ltd, Chippenham

Cover design by Tania Lambert
Cover pentacle designed by Kevin Saunders
(and inspired by the Enochian pentacle of Dr. John Dee)

ISBN 0 9542963 2 X

Details of courses run by the author Kevin Saunders
can be found on his website:

www.avalonweaver.com

GREEN MAGIC

CONTENTS

TABLE OF ILLUSTRATIONS, PHOTOS AND GRAPHICS

I'm waiting for the Angels of Avalon,
Waiting for the eastern glow.
The apples of the valley hold,
The seeds of happiness,
The ground is rich from tender care,
Repay do not forget!

Jimmy Page, Led Zeppelin, 1971.
(The Battle of Evermore)

1

INTRODUCTION

Wicca is a modern neopagan religion, or perhaps more accurately a spiritual framework with a pagan foundation, originally devised by Gerald Gardner through the 1940s and 50s. Gerald Gardner was a British witch with many years of experience who studied and practised a number of magical systems belonging to several traditions that had been developed through the ages. He had almost certainly been introduced to a form of traditional witchcraft back in the 1940s, probably in England's New Forest. With his experience in other occult paths it is apparent that he was able to see a great deal of value in the fragments of traditional witchcraft that had survived and the importance of its cultural integrity. However, due to centuries of persecution, with the Craft surviving as best it could underground, much of the material had been lost, as anyone who has tried to follow a truly traditional path will probably be aware, and what had survived clearly had become desperately fragmented. Gerald used his experience and knowledge of paths trod before him by organisations such as Freemasonry, the Golden Dawn, the Ordo Templi Orientis and Atlantian Adepts, to name but a few, and recreated a native British form of witchcraft he called Wicca. At the time Gerald Gardner was also working with a group of Druid revivalists, who were attempting to do much the same in different ways. Some of Gerald's earlier works were published in the 1950s, when witchcraft in England had only just become legal again, using his Druidic name of 'Scire'.

It is unlikely that Gerald Gardner and the many other talented people around him, such as Doreen Valiente, fully appreciated what he had started. Some of his writings suggest that he expected Wicca to fade away; instead it is fast becoming a system of spirituality and magic, based on ancient teachings, that is inspiring people around the world to work with the Goddess and God (or goddesses and gods)

1

once again. Wicca is possibly the fastest growing religion in the 21st Century. Despite being inspired by 'the old ways' it is as if spirituality has come full circle, with many people finding that Wicca provides the most suitable framework for a new spirituality that works in harmony with natural laws so desperately needed after centuries of environmental degradation and neglect.

During the 1960s, Wicca began to be developed further with the help of witches such as Doreen Valiente and Alex Sanders, to name but two. One of Gerald Gardner's students, Raymond Buckland, took Wicca to the USA where it has gained a strong foothold and is growing fast in its own fashion.

Wicca, as it was originally devised, is a group-oriented path where elders work with others in the group to gradually develop their skills and guide their growth as priestesses and priests in service to the Goddess and God. There has always been an encouragement to use Wicca as a broad framework, within which each individual must see things their own way and work with divinity, spirits and other energies as they feel is right. The framework itself offers a strong ethically sound basis, a general form of worship, and a system of three degrees that mark growth. Obviously, the success of any such system is heavily reliant on quality elders who guide newcomers through often emotionally painful personal growth experiences. Without quality teachers, Wicca will gradually degrade and become little more than is currently found in the many teen-witch journals and commercialised spell-weaving books now flooding the market. *Advanced Wiccan Spirituality* will help contribute towards ensuring that the deeper and more serious aspects of the Craft are not lost. It will help those who may have read some of the many beginners' books, including my own first book *Wiccan Spirituality*, to go one step further. It will also be of value to those who have spent some years working as Wiccans and who are now teaching and guiding others on the path. It is important to understand that whilst Wicca is still in its infancy, it is only natural that some aspects appear quite shallow, but that if those of us who take it seriously persevere, through working with our goddesses, gods, guides and other energies, Wicca will offer a magical path that has the potential to help change society for the good of all.

As Wicca has spread across the world, many new forms have been developed. This is good and should be encouraged in order to keep Wicca relevant to each group, to each culture, and to the times as they change. Any spiritual path that is immovably welded to dogma will simply not stand the test of time. However, I do feel it is important to maintain at least the broad original framework of Wicca otherwise there is a danger that it will gradually degenerate so far away from its original form that it becomes just a peculiar fad without depth. Wicca is not a solitary path but a group-oriented path. People developing a connection with the goddesses and gods on their own follow a worthy path, but it is not correct (in my view and in that of Wicca's founders) to describe such a path as Wicca. The term 'solitary Wicca' is basically a contradiction in terms and appears to have first been used by American authors who understandably preferred to use the term 'Wicca' instead of 'witchcraft' because of the intense resistance to and fears of such terms amongst the US Christian fraternity. All Wiccans, however, will find that they are often working alone, but it is the fact that they are working under the guidance of experienced elders, and therefore always have people to turn to for advice, that makes all the difference. I would emphasise here that I do not consider anything wrong with working as a solitary witch, and even if treading such a path there is a great deal in this book that will be of value, just that I consider it important to define what is meant as Wicca and what is meant as solitary.

RAINBOW WICCA

As I have already stated, it is in the nature of Wicca for it to develop in its own way. What I have endeavoured to do in this volume of *Advanced Wiccan Spirituality* is to look back at the original teachings on Wicca and ascertain the many influences that inspired Gerald Gardner. Having determined those influences I have used them within the framework of Wicca, as I understand and practise myself, to present a range of teachings and exercises that could be considered either a much needed revision, a deeper redevelopment of Wicca's many aspects, or even a completely new path in its own right. With my own emphasis on developing the depth of Wicca alongside an effort to keep it relevant to living in the 21st Century, no doubt many will consider it more of a new path. However, it is taken, I trust, that it will be accepted at face value. There is far too much navel gazing within Wicca in my opinion, far too much looking back at how things may have been done in the past, and too little emphasis on looking forward and its potential value to the future. It is my opinion that too many people involved in the Craft expend a great deal of time and effort in dissecting teachings and endeavouring to prove that a small detail is inaccurate, a form of intellectual snobbery, rather than looking at the big picture and welcoming the overall input. We can learn much from how things were done in the distant past, if indeed that can truly be ascertained, but we live in the 21st Century where much of what was done is no longer relevant. The entire human race has evolved in many ways over the past few thousand years and any new spiritual path that is going to help that evolution must surely keep up with the times.

There is much within Gerald Gardner's teachings that strongly suggest that he drew on the many developments being made throughout the early 20th Century by Theosophists who were borrowing much from middle and far eastern teachings, blending it with western thinking. With this in mind I have used much of the influences of Buddhist, Hindu and Judaic thinking with the seven planes of reality, depicted in various ways, coming to the fore to show the great depth that Wicca can offer when this is portrayed within a native Celtic framework. Using the seven colours of the rainbow that equate with these seven planes I have developed my own ways, from my Gardnerian roots, into a form of Wicca I call 'Rainbow Wicca'. Whatever form of Wicca you may choose to follow, whether it be my way, someone else's or your own, there will be much in this volume to inspire – at least that is the intention. That is something that, as with all things, only you can decide.

This volume deals with a great deal of information that will help those who aspire to make a valuable contribution to the work of the Goddess and God as a Priestess or Priest in their service. The material I have included intends to inspire and to offer suggestions on how further self-development in that direction can be achieved. There are no long lists of spells, as if all there were to working spells was reading from a recipe book, but if the material is digested and put into practice then the spells you work will almost certain gain in potency. There are no long lists of rituals, though the material will help you strengthen the rituals you undertake and help to give them greater depth. There are no lengthy examinations of ancient mythology, though mythology is important, but there are already many good books on this subject. What I have presented here in volume 1 of *Advanced Wiccan Spirituality* is material to inspire the aspirant, exercises to encourage practice, and revisions of Wicca suitable for the 21st Century that should help the Craft to maintain the depth of understanding it requires if it is going to continue to offer an alternative path to full union with the Divine.

2

WICCA'S ETHICAL BASIS

'Love is the law and love is the bond,
Merry do we meet, merry do we part,
And merry shall we meet again.'

Wicca is a spiritual framework for interacting with nature and the goddesses and gods that we experience as part of nature. It is not a passive path, but an active one. As such it is particularly important that we have, as its foundation, a sound ethical basis. Nature's energy can be used in many ways. Witchcraft is the active use of those natural energies. The energies of the lower planes can be utilised in many ways for the greater good or otherwise. It is therefore possible to be a 'witch', that is someone who manipulates these energies, for selfish motives that are not in tune with nature's imperative to grow and develop towards a higher state of existence on the physical plane. This would be what many might call 'black magic'. Wicca is, in the opinion of this author and that of its original founders, a system that has a strong ethical framework that is in tune with the highest spiritual values. As such, its ethical foundation is one that all witches would do well to adhere to if they are not to fall foul of the inescapable laws that affect everyone whether they believe in them or not. In reality, nature is neither black nor white. Black and white are but two poles representing positive and negative energies that need to work together if that energy is to flow and be productive. The path may lead in many directions, weaving in and out and from one pole to another, but whatever the path, they all lead to the same goal that sits between these two poles in harmony and in balance.

It should be pointed out here that Wicca is only one of many valid spiritual paths that eventually lead to one common truth. Other esoteric paths are equally valid, though there is most likely only one that is right for you. There is no right way or wrong way, just different ways.

Wiccans do not generally tend to accept many rules, though there have been attempts to introduce a whole range of restrictions of dubious value. It is usually recognised that life has to be experienced in many ways in order to eventually secure the connection with the Goddess and God and undertake the work of opening themselves up to serve them. There are, however, some fundamental guiding principles that are expressed through the Wiccan Rede – 'If it harm none, do what ye will'. This has been incorporated into a longer verse by the founders of Wicca as follows:

THE WICCAN REDE

Bide ye Wiccan laws ye must
in perfect love and perfect trust
Live and let live, fairly take, fairly give
Form the circle thrice about to keep all evil spirits out
To bind ye spell every time, let ye spell be spoke in rhyme
Soft of eye, light of touch, speak ye little, listen much
Deosil go by the waxing moon, singing out ye Witches' Rune
Widdershins go by the waning moon, chanting out ye Baneful Rune
When the moon rides at her peak, then ye heart's desire seek
Heed the North wind's mighty gale, lock the door and trim the sail
When the wind comes from the South, love will kiss thee on the mouth
When the wind blows from the West, departed souls may have no rest
When the wind blows from the East, expect the new and set the feast
Nine woods in ye cauldron go, burn them fast and burn them slow
Elder be ye Lady's tree, burn it not or cursed ye'll be
When the wheel begins to turn, soon ye Beltane fire'll burn
When the wheel hath turned to Yule, light a log the Horned One rules
Heed ye flower, bush and tree, by the Lady blessed be
Where the rippling waters flow, cast a stone and truth ye'll know
When ye have and hold a need, harken not to other's greed
With a fool no season spend, nor be counted as his friend
Merry meet and merry part, bright the cheeks and warm the heart
When misfortune is anow, wear the blue star upon thy brow
True in love ye must ever be, lest the love be false to thee
In these eight words the Wiccan Rede fulfil;
If it harm none, do what ye will.

The call 'If it harm none, do what ye will' is one that is often interpreted as a call to a form of anarchism inasmuch as it is understood to mean that one should do whatever one likes and enjoy life as one likes, as long as it doesn't seriously harm anyone. This is a very basic interpretation! It actually means far more than this. The 'will' does not refer to that of the lower self, it is not essentially a call to simply enjoy the simple things of life and satisfy the lower egotistical self, but refers to the will of the Higher Self. This is the 'will' that is touch with the Goddess and God whom Wiccans aim to serve as priestesses and priests of the Craft and is a far higher and more challenging calling that requires a great deal of discipline on the part of the lower self. It suggests that, if one is to progress to the point of becoming a High Priestess or High Priest, then the lower life needs to bow its head to the needs of the Goddess and God, to become in touch with the 'will' of the Higher Self that receives guidance from these spiritual energies. It often means that there is a need to undertake work that may not always satisfy the individual's lower nature that prefers merely to play and is, to some degree, selfish. When one becomes in touch with one's higher nature the inescapable connecting with everything and everyone around us becomes evident and what affects it and them will also affect the individual.

The strong ethical framework of Wicca is also found in the Law given to initiates at their first initiation which reads as follows…

> *'That you love all things in nature.*
> *That you shall suffer no person to be harmed by your hands or through your mind.*
> *That you walk humbly in the ways of your brothers and sisters and the ways of the gods.*
> *That you shall learn contentment through your suffering and from the nobility of mind and purpose.*
> *Remember that the wise never grow old, for their minds are nourished by living in the light of the gods.'*

This 'law' gives perhaps a more direct and less easy to misconstrue message to those entering Wicca, and a clue to the fact that service to the Goddess and God is not at all times an easy one, but that which requires effort and sacrifice. It is not a path for everyone, and not everyone is ready to serve in such an active, self-sacrificing way. There is nothing wrong if someone who approaches Wicca realises that they are not ready to take such a vow; in fact it would be foolish to push anyone when they are not ready. Many life experiences are required before people are ready to make such sacrifices and to undertake the esoteric disciplines that train them to actively serve effectively. Being passive and honouring the gods in a less active, yet still valuable, pagan way is perfectly understandable and the way in which many are moving as we approach the energies of the new age.

Law is the imposition upon the will of that which has a purpose beyond our full appreciation as incarnate mortals. The laws of nature have their higher spiritual counterparts. The best we can do as a race under the current circumstances is to learn how to love. By learning how to love everyone, no matter what creed, colour or race, to learn to love and respect one another and our Mother Earth, we will then be ready as a race to begin the next stage of development as the Age of Aquarius draws near.

A law that is recognised by witches, and ignored at their own peril, is the Three-fold Law. It states that whatever one gives out returns to the sender three times over. This is a natural law rather than a philosophical guiding principle and as such applies whether one believes in it or not.

It is also a law that seems to be much misunderstood, just as is the Wiccan Rede. On the face of it one may consider it to be a threat that if one were to undertake bad deeds then one will be a victim of that negativity as a punishment. Whilst it is true that the negativity will hit the perpetrator with three times the force of that which is originally put into the deed, it is not true that it is a punishment from some outside force. Once again, the truth lies within the individual. Any intentional negativity generated by a person will tend to stick in the mind of that person and affect them on a mental level. From the mental level it will filter through to affect them on a spiritual level and also on the physical level. It is as much a psychological process as a mystical one. It is the understanding of this law that ensures that the wise witch works for the common good rather than manipulating the powers of nature for personal gain at the expense of others, or to seek retribution for malice aimed at them. The wise witch recognising this law will simply protect themselves from any malice by ensuring that the negativity aimed at them is reflected directly back to the sender who themselves will suffer from the Three-fold Law with no effect on the intended target.

This law, of course, does more than merely protect oneself from negativity through such reflection, or teach the perpetrators of any such malice through the suffering of their own negativity. The law also works with positive energy. If a person dedicates their life to doing good deeds for those around them, or for the common good as a whole, that positive energy will also manifest through themselves on the mental, spiritual and physical level. So not only is it a law that discourages bad needs, it encourages and rewards good.

An aspect of witchcraft that is attractive to the immature within our materialistic culture, and one that is encouraged by a host of commercially orientated 'esoteric' writers, is the idea of being able to use the powers of nature to gain money or manipulate the love of a potential partner. One of the first things that a Wiccan undertakes on their path before they even reach the position of being initiated to the first degree, is to dedicate themselves to the Goddess and God within and to love and honour themselves as they would love and honour the gods. Without such a dedication, the potential initiate will fail to learn what witchcraft is all about and will thus be unable to fully tune themselves to the energies that they will later use to work magic of any great value.

Techniques of visualisation, backed up by the intent focused through the use of certain words (or 'spells' as they are generally presented) can have a certain degree of success, at least initially. If one calls on the gods for a wealth of money and enough energy is put into the visualisation and the intent, it may well be rewarded by some success. But it is highly unlikely that any money forthcoming will bring any great satisfaction. It is more likely to bring misery in the long run either by expecting to be continually rewarded with similar amounts of cash, and when it is no longer forthcoming suffering years of debts; or by the realisation that despite the promises made by the false gods worshipped in this modern world of materialism and unfettered commerce that money doesn't buy happiness. For many this is a hard but useful lesson if it is eventually appreciated.

Love may also be attracted by such methods with some degree of success. Equally hard lessons are likely to be learnt through such manipulation as the love attracted is unlikely to be based on anything deep and solid, but more often on something as fickle as lust. Such relationships, if they work at all, are doomed to failure, bringing the misery that is deserved through abusing the powers of nature. Love can be attracted to the individual only when it is not directed at a particular individual, but based on attraction based on being a sincerely nice, honest person who is confident and able to love themselves. If one cannot love oneself, how can anyone truly expect anyone else to love them?

Witches are taught that manipulation of others is something to be avoided at all costs. It is something that will almost certainly be subject to the Three-fold Law with the resulting self-punishment as the final product. There is no protection from this law, as it is a law of nature. To teach a young witch that they should never undertake any such manipulation is a vital guiding principle. They may well express despair and claim that if one can't use the magical powers of nature for personal gain then there is no point in being a witch. This is, however, merely an expression of their own immaturity and a sign that they are not ready to learn the ways of the occult – the hidden inner powers of the human mind. It is only natural that a young person reaching towards maturity and just discovering how their society and the world works should think like this; it is all part of growing up, but it is also the reason why any serious coven of witches should resist introducing anyone under the age of 18. Even at that age a good teacher should be careful to ensure that the individual is of an exceptionally mature mind with righteous intentions.

Some branches of Wicca, over the years, have adopted a whole string of laws, added by people such as Gardner and Sanders at a later date, that include a great deal of unnecessary and pointless dogma about how a coven should be run, etc. These I find quite spurious. Dogma should have no place in Wicca and the preceding laws of nature that I have detailed here, if applied properly, are more than adequate to suit all occasions in my experience.

FOUR FREEDOMS

Whilst not Wiccan, the words spoken by US President Franklin D Roosevelt would appear to fit very well into the ethics applied within Wicca on a global scale between nations. I have included these great words of inspiration, as simple as they are, in order to help inspire others who may share such a noble vision and care to help, in however a small way, to achieve this worthy ambition.

> '*In the future days, which we seek to make secure, we look forward to a world founded upon four essential human freedoms.*
>
> *The first is freedom of speech and expression – everywhere in the world.*
>
> *The second is freedom of every person to worship God in his own way – everywhere in the world.*
>
> *The third is freedom from want – which translated into world terms, means economic understandings which will secure to every nation a healthy peacetime life for its inhabitants – everywhere in the world.*
>
> *The fourth is freedom from fear – which, translated into world terms, means a worldwide reduction of armaments to such a point and in such a thorough fashion, that no nation will be in a position to commit an act of physical aggression against any neighbour – anywhere in the world.*'

3

JUNGIAN PSYCHOLOGY AND WICCA

*'Life, so-called, is a short episode between two
great mysteries, which are yet one.'*
– Carl Gustav Jung 1875–1961

A criticism that could be thrown at Wicca is that it is 'all psychology'. This is an understandable criticism in that psychology plays an important part if Wicca is taught well and its practical side of magic is to be thoroughly appreciated. 'Know thyself' is a fundamental starting point in any esoteric tradition and utilising an understanding of modern psychology is a good place to start to know yourself. However, it is a starting point, not an end in itself. Wicca generally uses psychology as an element of development, and an important pathway to self-knowledge, rather than the central theme of its entire approach. It is the pathway, not the destination. Magic, the transformation of energy from one form to another, can include an element of psychology but it is, at the same time, far more.

Wiccans do work with real astral, mental and spiritual entities. These are not psychological fantasies or limited to a wild imagination even though many illusions will inevitably present themselves as the aspirant gradually uncovers the veils. Psychological understanding leads to what lies beyond the contents of our physical brains rather than within its confines. Carl Gustav Jung was the first psychologist who took psychological understanding beyond the limit of scientific experimentation. He delved far into the mystical aspects of our existence, and his teachings certainly fit very snugly into the Wiccan ways. Wicca, however, takes Jung's teachings one stage further, within the framework of the culture to which we belong and alongside the addition of teachings that go back much farther. Wicca is, in many ways, a natural extension of

Jung's work, one of many possible extensions, and one that is as valid as any other.

FREUD AND JUNG

Jung was born in 1875 in Switzerland. He was a physician and a psychoanalyst and became one of Sigmund Freud's earliest and closest colleagues. Freud and Jung worked well together for many years. From an astrological perspective there was much between them that offered a perfectly complementary working relationship. Jung had his Sun in Leo and his Moon in Taurus, Freud had his Sun in Taurus. The Sun represents the lower self and the Moon the inner ego. With Freud's Sun being reflected in Jung's Moon, this allowed for a close relationship whilst Jung's ego reflected Freud's self. However, their Suns were squared, causing potential conflict. Despite their once close relationship, their differences eventually became irreconcilable causing them to go their separate ways in 1913.

Understandably they had developed many concepts in common, chiefly that of the conscious and subconscious parts of our psyche. There were, however, an ever increasing number of differences. Freud, for instance, saw 'God' as little more than a vast parental projection. Jung, on the other hand, had studied many esoteric traditions. He was a Christian Gnostic with a very open mind. Jung appears to have understood that consciousness exists before physical birth and therefore the psyche was quite distinct and far more than simply that contained within a physical body. Freud had a comparatively simplistic approach to psychology. As far as he was concerned there was a single correct development path that any individual should follow and that any deviation from his defined 'norm' would result in a neurosis that required correction. Jung, however, realised that to properly understand anyone's 'proper' development it was necessary to understand that different psychological types grow and develop in different ways. This understanding led Jung to develop a far more holistic approach to analysis.

EGO

The first concept that is useful to consider is one that we are all generally quite familiar with – ego. The word 'ego' itself is loaded with all sorts of individualised definitions which is something you need to watch out for.

▲ *Figure 1 – Aspects of the lower ego*

To some esotericists the *true* ego is that of the soul. For the purposes of this book we shall consider ego as the part of the lower self that contains a whole host of glamours and illusions that are evident on the physical and emotional planes (Figure 1).

The ego consists of two elements – the persona and the shadow. It can be useful to consider the image of a ball. The ball itself represents the ego. The side that you generally show to the outside world, how you would like to be seen, is the persona. The persona is how we present ourselves, what we allow others to see. To those who have nothing in the way of personal development the persona may actually be how they see themselves having not delved any deeper than what is apparent in the mirror. However, looking at our ball once again it is obvious that besides the half of the ball we can see there is also a half we cannot see. This is the shadow. It is just as much a part of us as the persona, but is the part we keep hidden, often even from ourselves. The shadow is where we bury all those bits we don't like about ourselves, and yet are actually an indivisible part. As a part of personal spiritual development, as a starting point, it is necessary to start looking at these things we have relegated to our shadow side, to examine it, to come to terms with it, to resolve the issues, and to feel entirely comfortable with it. This is easier said than done. If at first you don't succeed (and if you find it rather easy to do I would suggest that perhaps you are still hiding something away) then take some solace from the fact that even some of the most advanced practitioners of the Craft have not entirely managed to come to terms with everything.

However hard it may be, it is necessary to fully incorporate the shadow and accept it as a part of ourselves that we cannot escape. Once we come to terms with our shadow, and can see where certain driving forces come from. We are able to gradually find an escape route from the illusions that we hold dear to ourselves, and the egotistical fantasies that we present to the world that form the foundation of the persona

13

we have adopted and which in turn can effectively manipulate others into bolstering our own fanciful glamours. In esoteric terms, the 'shadow' is often what is referred to as 'the Dweller on the Threshold'. To move beyond this threshold we need to confront this dweller, and only then can we successfully begin to explore the realms beyond.

As a clear example I can think back to an old friend of mine who was potentially a wonderful and powerful High Priestess. She spent her time sharing words of wisdom with others across the Internet and had built up an elaborate victim fantasy that worked well in getting the emotional attention and sympathy that she craved. Unfortunately, those who got to know her closely soon realised that, whilst there were things in her past that were very painful, they were not as elaborate as that which had built up. She didn't like people finding this out, didn't like people getting close enough to uncover the truth, because to face and resolve these issues meant removing the element within her persona that brought so much sympathy from others – and that was something too highly valued to let go of. So rather than resolving these issues she simply spent her time building up the victim fantasy even further. This worked very well for her amongst her circle of friends and, as long as she could keep them from getting too close, but was no substitute for facing reality and reaching towards freedom and enlightenment.

In esoteric terms the ego belongs to the lower emotional (otherwise known as astral) plane. The shadow side needs to be fully faced and incorporated before growth can successfully continue towards the mental and spiritual planes that lie beyond the lower and higher emotional planes. The shadow is where we tend to hide all our animal and sexual instincts and other things we have repressed from our persona due to pressures from our ego ideal and the expectations of modern society. Continual repression of our shadow self can result in denial, blocked energies, pent up anger or aggression, depression, etc. In severe cases it can even result in a bi-polar type of disorder. The shadow side can build up a head of steam that suddenly explodes and lead to some serious psychological problems. For this reason it is wise to approach any work on the shadow self with a certain amount of caution and if you are involved in guiding others through this process you will need to learn to push but not to push too hard. Let the pressure valve open slowly so that any unresolved issues can be dealt with one at a time as they arise. Suppressed pain (and sometimes rage) is often quite ugly when exposed to the light!

Projection is a Jungian concept that you may become familiar with. It is a technique used by many of us at a sub-conscious level where we project our own faults, those we have buried so deep in our shadow side that we deny them, onto those around us. What we judge or condemn is often what we do not accept ourselves within our own self. When we criticise others we should be aware that what we are judging may not be in them but from within the shadow side of ourselves that we are projecting onto them. The darkness you see in others may actually be closer than you think! Symptoms of projection include the perpetuation of feuds (often within family or friends); destructive obsessions that appear to have no reason; branding others as scapegoats from society's ills; or blaming other people for your own problems. It is also important to remember that that problems in others are not always the cause of projection...there are times when these problems really do exist in them, but you do need to look deep within yourself to be able to make the distinction.

PSYCHOLOGICAL TYPES

Jung's definition of psychological types is one where the (unintended) links with Wicca come into their own. He defined four main types, each of which could be expressed in either introvert or extrovert ways – making a total of eight. The four basic psychological types are 'thinking', 'intuitive', 'feeling', and 'sensate'. They can be arranged on a chart as shown Figure 2. This shows the four main psychological types arranged around a quartered circle with sensate opposite intuitive and feeling opposite thinking. It also shows the correspondences – sensate to earth, thinking to air, intuitive to fire, and feeling to water – and see

▲ *Figure 2 – Main psychological function types*

15

that they are arranged in a fashion that all Wiccans will recognise as the elements found around a fully cast circle in there correct positions and this is something we can use during the development process.

Jung determined that we each have a main psychological function that falls somewhere within this circle of attributes. He also determined that we have a main function, two secondary functions and an inferior function. The main function flanks the two inferior functions and is always opposite the inferior function (Figure 3). Therefore, if your main function is thinking (i.e. you are an air type) then your secondary functions are sensate and intuitive, and your inferior function is feeling. You should be most comfortable whilst working with your main function, you will most likely not have too much trouble dealing with work on your secondary functions, but you will find it most difficult working with your inferior function. This does not mean that your inferior function does not exist, but it does mean that your inferior function is what you feel most uncomfortable with and are likely to have buried it deep in your shadow self. If you are a thinking type, someone who bases everything on logic, then the emotional feeling function will be easily dismissed as something that is inferior as it will be considered illogical.

There is nothing 'wrong' with being any one of these types – expressed either introvertly or extrovertly – it's just the way we are and part of the broad diversity that makes us human. However, it is very useful to be able to step back and judge accurately and objectively where we fall within this spectrum of psychological types. One of the advantages of working with a teacher in a group-oriented path is that your teacher will find it much easier to offer an objective opinion about you than you will yourself.

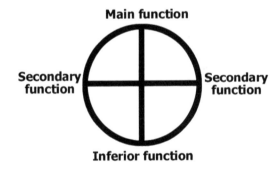

▲ *Figure 3 – Your inferior function is always opposite your main function*

The functions can be seen as the manifestation of the elements as they work through ourselves. In reality, not everyone is going to fall squarely within any one of the functions any more than everyone falls directly into the full influence of any astrological sign (and here there is a relationship as we will explore later in this book). You may find that your main function falls somewhere between any two, but your inferior function (or shadow function) will always be opposite. If you are a strong air type, then you will find it hard to understand strong water types and vice versa. If you are a strong earth type you will find it hard to understand a strong fire type. You may, however, find that the partner you end up with and get on best with, is the complete opposite of your own type. Opposites often do either repel strongly or attract. By finding a partner of the opposite type you can both bring the much needed balance into your lives. By attracting a partner of the same type, especially if it is strong in nature, this is often a sign that balance has not being achieved and that there is much of the inner self being denied. In such a situation you could be simply finding the easy way out and bolstering the attraction to your own ego.

When you also bring in the introvert and extrovert dimension, you will find that if your psychological type is expressed as, for example, an introverted feeling type, then the function most unlike how you see yourself would be the extroverted thinking type. In fact, when you come across a person who is diametrically opposite your own type you will most likely either dislike them intensely or fall in love. In the first instance it will be because you sub-consciously see in them all the things you have buried away in yourself that you are not ready to face, in the second, you will recognise your complementary opposite (that you actually have inside yourself) that helps you to feel whole and complete.

Our aim, as part of our development programme in Wicca (something that should normally be undertaken between the first degree and the second), is to balance these elements within ourselves and start working at incorporating our shadow. One of the reasons it is useful to work under the guidance of a High Priestess or High Priest is that they have (or should have) been through this process, are able to recognise your needs, and should be able to gently guide you through the process with the benefit of being more objective than you are able to be about yourself. You are, of course, likely to have to face many things along the path that you find unpleasant about yourself. There may be times when your High Priestess or High Priest metaphorically has to hold up a mirror for you to look in, one in which you see those things you don't like, and this is one of the reasons you choice of High Priestess and/or High Priest needs to be a careful one. It is one of the reasons why you must only work with people you truly approach with perfect love and perfect trust. If not you will find yourself in a position of vulnerability that (without the trust) leaves you open to abuse.

THE THINKING TYPE

Thinking (or air) types thrive on logic and order. The inferior function is feeling and for this reason emotions are hard to accept as they get in the way of logic and order. To someone who is a feeling type, thinking types will most likely feel very cold-hearted at times. Thinking types tend to be quite emphatic in their definitions of what is good or bad, it is either one or the other with nothing in between. There are few shades of grey. They tend to be very tidy people in one way or another with everything packed into boxes which in the extrovert thinking type can mean literally, or the introvert thinking type on a mental level.

Because thinking types like rules, their morality can be extremely rigid. There is rarely much room for human fallibility in their strict code as they tend to see everything in black and white. Unfortunately the real world is full of human fallibilities and rarely fits in completely with the idealistic values of the thinking type.

When the inferior function of feeling does make its way to the surface from the shadow side it can reveal exceptionally tender emotions that rupture intensely having been so deeply repressed.

THE INTUITIVE TYPE

Intuitive (or fire) types tend to be those who are always looking forward, the past has little interest but the future is full of possibilities, even the present is only of interest from the perspective of what it brings about. They always seem to have a great sense of how things will pan out, no matter how complex the influences, and are thus often just one step ahead of everyone else. When expressed in an extrovert way this can make them the leaders of fashion, they can also be a little like social butterflies flitting from one group of friends to another. Introvert intuitive types can be great visionaries, prophets and mystics and, if expressed through art or poetry, this can appear quite abstract with little attention to detail.

As the inferior function of an intuitive is the earthy sensate function they often deal very badly with the material things of the world. They may have little regard for money, food, sexual relationships, home, etc. They are so engrossed in the future possibilities of things they can lose touch with the present altogether.

THE FEELING TYPE

The feeling (or water) type tends to live on his or her emotions and put great store in memories comparing current situations with the past. To a thinking type they can appear quite fluffy and illogical. They tend to be very understanding people with infinite grades of value and always understanding why a person might feel the way they do.

Extroverted feeling types tend to be everyone's friend. They can be totally at ease in any given social situation. They may have built up many friendships as they tend to be far more willing to say what those around them want to hear rather than what they are actually thinking. Introverted feeling types are difficult to get through to as their feelings run deep and yet they rarely express those feelings, preferring to keep them to themselves – still waters run deep!

When the inferior thinking function does rise to the surface, the feeling type can come up with some painfully accurate conclusions having been able to feel to the very depth of an issue then being able to apply logic. This may only happen occasionally – be prepared to be stunned when it does.

THE SENSATE TYPE

Sensate (or earth) types are the great realists with their feet always firmly in the earth. They will most likely consider the whole idea of intuition as complete nonsense, preferring to believe in what they see before them as the only thing of any value. They tend to get their vision of the world through measuring its physical data. They tend to be very good and sensible with money and may be very materialistic.

The extrovert sensate will tend to adjust easily to any given situation. They do not have any great expectations and accept things as they are at any given moment. Introvert sensate types might express themselves in very matter of fact terms; if through art, then they will paint or draw what they see.

When the shadow side shows itself, sensate types can find themselves engrossed in the unfamiliar territory of intuition whilst offering great resistance and going along with a current fad, but will soon pull themselves out of it once they ground themselves again. They are not generally very good at applying their inner experiences to their outer lives.

EXERCISE – YOUR PSYCHOLOGICAL TYPE

Lay out a circle with green, yellow, red and blue candles marking the quarters as you would when preparing to cast a standard Wiccan Circle. Place items in front of each of these candles that are associated with those elements. These could be the witch's tools such as the pentacle, athame, wand and chalice, or you could use crystals, flowers, personal items, ornaments, etc. When you are ready, light the candles and, being as objective as you can, stand near the edge of the circle, facing the centre, where you feel your own psychological type fits best. Remember that you will not necessarily fall precisely into earth, air, fire or water, you may well fit half way between two.

When you have decided where you stand look at the items that lay around the circle on the edge directly opposite you. These objects or items will be those that most closely associate with your inferior function. Cross the circle and work with those items for a while and make a log of how you felt throughout the process.

If you have a partner, try getting both of you to see where you fit around the circle and, when you have both decided what psychological types you are, see how these might relate to each other. If you are opposite each other, do you bring balance to each of your personalities? If you are in the same place, do you complement each other in different ways? Make a note in your logs.

MASTERING THE ELEMENTS

In Wicca, as in other occult/esoteric traditions, part of the growth process involves mastering the 'elements'. In Wicca they are known as Earth, Air, Fire and Water. But what does this mean? It is often presented as something entirely mysterious, but in fact it can be explained, in general terms, in a reasonably simple way. Water represents our emotions. Therefore to master our inner water element would require us to master our emotions, master them so that we gain balance and control over them so our emotions do not rule us. The same applies to all of the other elements. To master them is not to 'master' in such a way as to suggest being a dictator, but rather as one who may master an instrument – with practice, with care, and with respect. It will be easy to master the elements associated with your primary function, reasonably easy to master those of your secondary functions, and take a great deal of work (potentially over many years) to master the elements associated with your inferior function.

Having mastered the elements within oneself, it is then possible to master those elemental forces of a similar but broader nature outside of the self. The elements are basically those forces that are most prevalent in the world of form. Mastering is about taking control, finding balance and rising above the elements – a matter of psychological and spiritual growth, but also a key to working as a witch, whether a wise one or not. It is entirely possible to work with the elements for selfish ends, to work negative magic against those you may consider to be 'enemies' as they have no set agenda other than to be available for use to help teach the lessons we all need in order to grow. Those who do use these forces for selfish 'needs' or in negative ways do learn – the hard way! Ever remember the Three-fold Law.

The elements found in the outer world of form each have a hierarchy of spirits associated with them. These can take the form of fairies (air), ondines (water), salamanders (fire) and gnomes (earth) although different people experience them in different ways and often have different names for them. No matter what they are called they are the same. You may find that the easiest way to experience these elementals is to practise tuning into them in nature when you can find a quiet spot to be on your own. Sacred places are particularly strong and often incorporate elements of a more highly developed nature being higher up the hierarchy. There are many good books on elemental spirits and – it must be said – a large number of not very good ones. The best advice is to experience them for yourself without too many preconceptions. Keep your mind open and let them come to you in their own way.

The elements belong to the lower planes, though the spirits directing them work on higher planes. Many people seem to restrict their magical work to working with the elements, and this is certainly a stage that is hard to avoid, but it is only a lower stage in the growth process, not an end in itself – it is part of the journey, not the destination. Working with the elements is something like learning to drive a car. You need to respect the power of the car, you need to appreciate how much damage you can do driving half a ton of metal at high speed, but you also need to remember that you are in control at all times, or should be. You cannot blame the car if something goes wrong any more than you can ask for it to do something. Learning this control is one of the most important tasks of working as a first degree Wiccan and it is advisable not to move beyond this stage of initiation until a reasonable degree of mastery has been attained and maintained.

ANIMA AND ANIMUS

In Jungian terms the anima is the personification of all the (often hidden) feminine attributes within a man and the animus is the personification of all the masculine attributes within a woman. I prefer to think of it in terms of each of us having both an anima and animus, one of which is hidden to a certain degree. In my experience with teaching, women don't tend to have much of a problem accepting that they have masculine attributes within. Men, however, often resist the idea that they have feminine attributes and refuse to accept the whole idea for fear that it may in some way challenge their masculinity. Whether it is accepted or not it's there (sorry guys!) and working at uncovering these attributes, no matter how deeply buried they are, is highly beneficial in the growth process.

ARCHETYPES

Archetypes are buried deep within ourselves. We are born to respond to various archetypal energies as part of our survival strategy, first with the basics such as Mother and Father, then later to more elaborate archetypes.

We have a certain set of archetypes that are inherited through the cultural group to which we belong. If the blood line which you are born into includes the Celtic goddesses and gods, then you will tend to more readily feel attracted to those important inherited forms. If you are born into a different blood line then those cultural archetypes may well be of another form, maybe Norse, Saxon, Egyptian, Hindu, etc. Whatever cultural grouping they belong to, there tend to be archetypes that fit into various types albeit with different names. These forms are inhabited by real higher spiritual energies and affect us on every plane. They are generally the same forces that play a part in other mythological sets, just in different guises.

Other archetypal models are also inherited and stimulated to consciousness through story telling. The Celtic myths such as the stories of Arthur, Merlin, Gwynevere, Morgan le Fay, etc. are all such models. It is easy to stimulate these archetypal energies to the point where they take over your whole lower egotistical self in the mistaken belief that this is your true higher self. Such people may have been aiming in the right direction, but missed the mark. How many people are there who believe they are the reincarnation of Merlin, Arthur or Morgan le Fay amongst the neopagan community?

Archetypal energies, within Wicca, can take many forms. They can be the gods and goddesses, they can also be the spirits of animals, trees, elementals, etc. Within a fully cast Circle, the High Priestess often is involved in a ritual called 'Drawing Down the Moon'. This involves the High Priest invoking the archetypal energies of the Moon Goddess, in any one of Her aspects (usually the full moon), into the High Priestess. The success of such an invocation will depend partly on the skill of the High Priest, but mainly on the connection the High Priestess has with the Goddess. Strictly speaking, in order to have become a High Priestess, this should be a highly developed connection. The High Priestess then, for the remainder of the ritual, undertakes the role of the Goddess personified having raised that archetypal energy into form as best she can. It is, however, important to remember that this invocation is released at the end of the ritual.

CONSCIOUS, SUBCONSCIOUS AND COLLECTIVE UNCONSCIOUS

Within psychology, the elements of the conscious mind and the subconscious mind, with all the ways each element affects each other is well established. It is generally accepted that every individual builds up a whole wealth of experience that can be buried deep within the subconscious that can be brought to the surface when required. The subconscious can also be the place where anything that the individual does not understand, or finds difficult to accept, is buried and ignored. These threads of misunderstanding, unacceptability or miscomprehension tend to float around the subconscious and often begin to attach themselves to other threads that have some common link and form complexes. These complexes in turn, as they become more and more elaborate, can affect the conscious mind with the individual fully appreciating where they come from and in the most severe instances these can lead to problems that cause serious psychological damage.

Spiritual development, whether it is along a Wiccan path, one of the other esoteric pagan paths, or through any number of other spiritual paths that are all valid within their own cultural frameworks, can help the individual delve into the realm of the subconscious. This exploration helps to provide reason where before there was none, to provide understanding where there was previous misunderstanding, and helps to unravel those subconscious threads that, instead of building up and causing problems, add to and broaden the conscious appreciation of the greater reality that lays beyond the material plane. The exoteric traditions, of which in our own culture Christianity in its conventional sense is the greatest example, deny this inner teaching and thus deny spiritual development of any degree, reserving the inner teachings for those whom the hierarchy deem worthy. The vast majority within these exoteric traditions are left in ignorance to a large degree. Whilst not wishing to knock Christianity in any great way, for under the surface its teachings are based on much the same as many older pagan teachings, I must question the wisdom of leaving people in ignorance and preventing the majority access to the deeper understanding that would benefit the whole of humanity.

The concept of the collective unconscious, or super-conscious, is one that is perhaps where Jung more often diverges from other branches of psychology, and diverges in the direction of those of the many occult paths. It refers to the universal source of mental consciousness that can be tapped into that appears to lay outside of the normal parameters of an individual mind. The super-conscious, by definition, suggests that there is a huge source of material to which every individual has access, consciously or subconsciously. This is something that the occultist tends to accept as a natural fact and the scientist cannot accept for lack of tangible evidence. The tangible evidence needed to satisfy the material scientist can never be satisfied because such realities, as with many of the occult realities, exist beyond tangibility.

4

SYMBOLS

Symbols have been used throughout history from the distant past to the present day, and no doubt will continue to be used in the future, because they offer us a graphic representation that is often easier for us to comprehend than mere words alone. Jung ascertained that messages tend to reach our conscious mind initially in the form of symbols from our subconscious. When we dream we dream in pictures and symbols, not generally in words. Understanding those symbols and where they come from can help us to understand ourselves, as long as we bear in mind that each of us is unique. Whilst there are culturally embedded symbols that are often common to all within that culture, there can also be symbols that, through personal experience, have gained a personal meaning, so whilst dream dictionaries may offer some guidance it is not wise to rely on them wholesale.

Religions throughout history have always used symbols to represent various archetypes, concepts and understandings that have been interpreted, reinterpreted (and often misinterpreted) as the years have passed by. Esotericists of most, if not all, paths tend to accept symbols as useful tools for building a necessary understanding and thereby reaching the energies in the other planes by opening up a channel through the conscious and subconscious mind. Once a channel is opened the communication becomes two-way. Once the messages coming through the sub-conscious to the conscious mind have been rightly understood, symbols can then be used in return to send messages back in turn to that which lies beyond the veil. This channel does not stop within the mind, conscious or sub-conscious, but reaches what psychologists might call the 'super-conscious' state.

The symbols I have chosen to examine here are either directly related to Wicca or come from a closely related source that has, in some way or another, influenced Wicca and its development. You may

25

well find, throughout your own practice, that you come across symbols that feel important to you. You may not, at the time, fully appreciate why, but in such circumstances it is often helpful to keep a record of it in some way and research it later. The full meaning will usually become clear in meditations or, at some point, your guides will thrust its understanding at your feet in some way.

THE PENTACLE

I have, of course, to start with the symbol most instantly recognisable as being associated with paganism, witchcraft and Wicca (along with a great many misconceptions too!) the pentacle (Figure 4). A pentacle is a pentagram inside a circle. The five points represent the 'five elements' of earth, air, fire, water and spirit. Spirit is associated with the uppermost point when drawn in its upright position. The pentagram (Figure 5) is normally drawn with an unbroken line. The point and direction at which one starts to draw the pentagram is significant. When drawn from the uppermost point one starts with spirit, the least dense of all the elements, then (drawing in a clockwise direction) you pass through fire, air, water and earth – each time working through an element denser than the previous one.

The points normally touch the inside of the outermost circle. The circle represents the continuous cycle of life with no beginning or end.

The pentagram, or five-pointed star, has a long history. Its first known use dates back to around 3500 BCE when it was known to be in use in Mesopotania. Greek Pythagoreans considered the pentagram's geometric qualities to represent both mathematical, and metaphysical, total perfection. Hidden within the geometry is the Phi ratio that

▲ *Figure 4 – Pentacle*

▲ *Figure 5 – Pentagram*

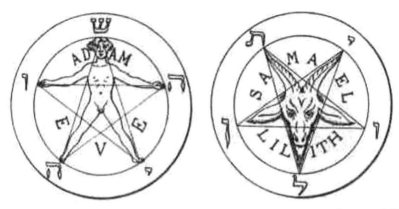

▲ *Figure 6 – Illustration attributed to the 19th Century Eliphas Levi, first recorded in 1961*

forms the basis of the Fabian Spiral – the golden mean. The Hebrews used the five-pointed star to represent a book in their bible, the Book of Penta-teuch. The symbol has also been used in the past by Christians though many will deny this. The five points represented the five wounds of Christ on the cross and it was used by the Christian Roman Emperor Constantine, the founder of the Catholic Church, as his seal and amulet.

The pentacle also finds its way into the Arthurian mythology. Sir Gawain, a nephew of Arthur and a knight of the round table, used a gold pentacle with a red background on his shield. In this respect it repre-sented the five knightly virtues of generosity, courtesy, chastity, chivalry and piety.

In its downward pointing position it is recorded to have been used by the Knights Templar who were demonised and excommunicated by the Roman Church like so many before them. The symbol they used was said to represent Baphomet, supposedly a pagan god of darkness. It was the horned god, or the goat-head god, that has been popularised through the Church as an image of their devil or satan. The Templars, once the warrior heroes of the Christian crusades, some say guardians of the Holy Grail, fell out of favour not just because of failures at war, but because they dared to uphold the early Gnostic Christians' (i.e. the more esoterically oriented early Christians before Rome gained political control) practice of worshipping the Goddess as well as the God. The Romans had decided that the feminine must be relegated and held in abeyance.

The name 'Baphomet' is interesting. If written in Hebrew and a simple code is applied to it, one ends up with the word for Sophia.

Sophia is the Christian Gnostic Goddess of Wisdom. So the Templars were worshipping an image with a masculine god image within which is hidden the name of the Goddess. As in Wicca and many pagan paths they were seen as two sides of the same coin.

More recently, it was adopted by the Church of Satan by group of people in the USA in the rebellious 1960s. It has since then, especially in the USA, become associated with Satanism although as an antithesis of the Christian Church, Satanism was more commonly associated with in inverted cross. Satanism, it should be noted, has nothing to do with witchcraft, Wicca, or paganism in its commonly-used modern sense.

Wiccans in the USA often avoid the inverted pentagram, because of the misconceptions of the non-pagan community. However, the inverted pentagram, as shall be seen in the chapter on the Kaballah, is rightly included as part of Wicca, as part of the original initiation rituals (and for good reason) as symbolic of second degree of development. In its reversed position it denotes (amongst other things that need to be considered) the initiate's connection with the five elements; however, the element of spirit is still not master of those elements. To attain third degree the initiate should symbolically signify this by mentally moving the element of spirit into its proper position, master over elements, ruled by spirit rather than being ruled by its lower self. The downward pointing pentagram or pentacle is therefore a useful and legitimate symbol for use in Wicca. We should do our best to reclaim it and educate people as to what it symbolises for us as best we can to foster further understanding rather than to reject it because of the in-built fears inherent in Christianity.

The pentagram is the symbol of the magician as a person who can fully understand and work magic utilising the elements of nature in balance with and mastered by the spirit. This ability is within all of us, therefore it is known as the sign of the microcosm, as it is in the macrocosmic world all around us. The elements of the Universe find equilibrium as they are mastered by the laws of the Universal Spirit. The pentagram, therefore, wielded by one who works in tune with those universal laws of nature, is one of the most potent symbols that exist.

If one draws a pentagram within a thirteen foot circle, with the points just touching the circle's circumference (forming a pentacle), the length of any one of the five straight lines forming the pentagram will measure 12.364 feet. (Obviously this works whatever unit is used – I suggest feet as this would provide a good working size for a cast Circle.) 12.364 is the precise number of lunar months in a solar year. Using the Celestial Circle casting method detailed later in this book, where a pentagram is cast within a thirteen foot circle, is a particularly appropriate method to use for honouring the Moon at an esbat ceremony.

The pentagram is closely associated with the planet Venus. This planetary energy has been assigned various goddess names in Her time including Venus, Aphrodite, Rhiannon and Mary to name but a few. If Venus's movement around the Sun is plotted, from the perspective from our planet, a perfect pentagram pattern can be traced. A remarkable coincidence?

THE HEBREW INTERPRETATIONS OF THE PENTAGRAM

Perhaps some of the most interesting interpretations (and ones partly adopted by other paths including Wicca) can be found amongst the Hebrew interpretations of the pentagram. The original Hebrews also saw the points on the pentagram as representing four elements of God (two masculine elements and two feminine elements) with the uppermost point representing spirit.

The four Hebrew letters around the lower points of the pentagram (Figure 7) are Yod, He, Vau, He. These are the four letters (equating to sounds or vibrations) that spell out what is known as the true name of God in Hebrew – YHVH – pronounced Yah We Yah Veh, or more commonly Jehovah. We need to remember that Hebrew is written from right to left, so YHVH is put on the pentagram from the bottom right working anti-clockwise.

The symbol at the top, in the position of spirit, is Shin (or Sin). This Hebrew letter is used to give an S or Sh sound. As in Wicca, it represents the divine spirit (notice its triple aspect). As the Sh sound, it also represents a higher occult secret. We also have here, perhaps, a clue as to the true meaning of sin that found its way into Christianity (that of course is an

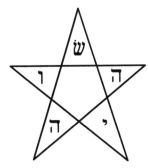

▲ *Figure 7 – Pentacle with Hebrew letter associations*

off-shoot of Judaism) but that is more often than not completely misunderstood by that faith. Sin or Shin in its position at the top of the pentagram represents the divine spirit following through the unbroken line of the figure through the other energies that form the name of God. If we now drop the Shin letter from its position in the spiritual plane into the position of the earthly material plane, i.e. into the middle of YHVH, we get the word YHSVH or Joshuah, or perhaps even more commonly known as Jesus. Jesus then is the representation of God on the physical plane and Sin is that element of the divine spirit when it is trapped in the material.

On the Tree of Life, the left hand column is associated with passive energies and the right hand column is associated with active energies. These are often (certainly in Wicca) seen as feminine (left) and masculine (right) which is why a Wiccan altar has the dark Goddess candle on the left and the bright God candle on the right. On the Tree of life, Keter (at the uppermost point) can be associated with a masculine aspect of God (Shek) and Malkut (at the lowermost point) with a feminine and earthly aspect of Goddess (Shekinah). We therefore have four general aspects of the divine represented above and below, and left and right (forming a cross configuration as in the Celtic Cross). As mentioned above, the letters forming the Hebrew word for God – YHVH – actually represent two masculine aspects and two feminine aspects (the two H's being feminine). They are also associated with elements of Earth, Air, Fire and Water. Yod to Fire, the first He to Water, Vau to Air, and the second He to Earth. If we remember that Hebrew is written from right to left and thus appear on the pentagram as in Figure 7 we can then see that these elements are placed in the way occultists of many breeds (including Wiccans) use them, as in Figure 8. This is how they have come to be handed down through time in those positions

You will, from this interpretation, also be able to see that there are two elemental aspects relating to God, one active and one passive, and two aspects relating to Goddess, also one active and one passive. This also corresponds with the Wiccan system where Earth and Water are associated with the Goddess, with Fire and Air being associated with the God.

There are further associations relating YHVH to the Kabbalah. There are four divisions of the planes – physical, emotional (or astral), mental and spiritual (we divide the upper three into lower and upper to give us the seven planes). In the Kabbalist system these are given the names of Assiah (physical), Atziluth (emotional), Yetzirah (mental), and Briah (spiritual). We can then see with this association, that we

▲ *Figure 8 – The positioning of the elements on the pentagram are defined by the Hebrew placing of YHSVH*

have a Goddess and God on the lower two planes, and a Goddess and God on the upper two. In Wicca we have many names for the aspects of Goddess and God. They can be reasonably be divided into those more clearly associated with the physical and emotional planes and those with more distant planes. The Earth Goddess, for instance, is sometimes known as Aradia, and the spirit of the forests, and Earth God might be associated with the horned one such as Cernnunos. Equally, the less earth bound Goddess could include Dana (as the moon) or Arrianrhod (as Queen of the Heavens) with perhaps Lugh or Bel (Solar deities) representing the God.

To finish this revelation of these links with Hebrew, the final association links us back to the Wheel of the Year. Each of the God and Goddess aspects represented by YHVH are associated with the four fixed signs in the Zodiac relating to each of those elements. Some of these associations can be seen more clearly in Table 1.

THE PENTAGRAM IN ISLAM

In 339 BCE Philip of Macedon (father of Alexander the Great) was prevented from conquering Byzantium (Constantinople, currently known as Istanbul) because his army's approach was spotted thanks to the light of a bright crescent moon. Byzantium, which had been dedicated to the Goddess Diana, used her symbol – the crescent moon – to represent the City. Later, when Emperor Constantine took over the City, he rededicated it to the virgin Mary. At that time Mary's symbol

Table 1 – *Associations of YHVH*

English	Hebrew	Form	Element	Alchemical symbol	Zodiac symbol	Zodiac name	Plane
Y	Yod	'	Fire	△	♌	Leo	Briah
H	He	ה	Water	▽	♍	Scorpio	Yetzirah
V	Vau	ו	Air	◬	≈	Aquarius	Atziluth
H	He	ה	Earth	▽	♉	Taurus	Assiah

was the pentagram as she had taken over the attributes of the pagan Venus (also symbolised by the pentagram). The five-pointed star was then added alongside the crescent moon. This emblem survived various invasions of the City and was first raised above Constantinople by Muslims in 1453 CE after its capture by Mahomet II. Since then, the crescent moon and pentagram symbol has been increasingly used by Muslims to identify themselves with variations of it appearing on a number of national flags of predominantly Muslim countries.

EXERCISE – USING THE PENTAGRAM TO ENERGISE THE BODY

This is a particularly useful and powerful way to start the day and helps to set the mood for living closely with the Goddess, God and the elements. It can be done at anytime if you so choose, or if you feel the need for a little energy, and can be conducted using the Sun or the Moon, but it is something I tend to do soon after getting out of bed to set me up for the day ahead.

Ideally, you need to stand either outside or in front of a window facing East at sunrise. It is best done skyclad, but this may not be practical (the windows I have facing East face the main road through the village, so I do not tend to stand in front of it naked for fear of causing an accident by a passing motorist!) First of all, bow respectfully to the rising Sun. Then, using your power hand, point towards the Sun and visualise His energy gathering on the tip of your finger. When you have felt the energy gather, slowly bring the tip of your finger to the brow of your head and feel the energy flow into your third eye. This tends to wake you up with a bit of a start so do it slowly and gently! Next, move your finger, still feeling the energy flowing, diagonally across your body to your left hip, then to your right shoulder, across to your left shoulder, down to your right hip, and finally

---

back to your brow again. Then stand for a few moments and breathe deeply. You have, in this way, drawn an active pentagram of spirit onto (and into) your body with the energy of the rising Sun. Notice by referring to Figure 9 that your heart centre falls in the middle of the pentagram when drawn this way.

Having completed this exercise you are probably in an ideal state to undertake your morning meditations.

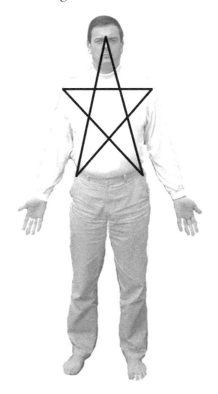

▲ *Figure 9 – Invoking the energies into the body using a pentagram*

THE HEXAGRAM

The hexagram (Figure 10) is also a symbol with a long history. It is worth remembering here that whilst Wicca was based on the fragments of traditional witchcraft that survived over the years, its founders had the wisdom to pull together the missing pieces by going back to the roots of that tradition thus giving it depth. The Celts ended up in Britain having migrated across Europe (over many hundreds of years) from

▲ *Figure 10 – The Hexagram*

the Eastern Mediterranean and, it is believed, contacts were maintained between Celtic Druid priests with the same region including Greece and Egypt.

To the Jews, the hexagram is most commonly known as *The Star of David*. It is also known as *The Seal of Solomon*, and is used as such within several Christian mystical paths, including Freemasonry. However, to the Hindu it is known as *The Star of Vishnu* (Vishnu is a Solar deity, or a solar aspect of Krishna). Once again we see a symbol being used by a wide variety of traditions and symbolising much the same attributes, albeit with varying terminology. This indicates, or at least strongly suggests, that there is a common source.

The six-pointed star is basically two interlocking triangles, one pointing up and the other pointing down. It represents the ultimate trilogy in duplicate – as above, so below; the macrocosm and the microcosm combined. In other words it symbolises what is seen as manifesting as the God and Goddess in the outside world and that which is replicated within us all. It can also be used to represent the upward triangle of spiritual fire mingling with the downward triangle of the primordial waters and thereby the flow of spiritual energy through matter.

The hexagram is the combination of the downward pointing triangle given to a witch at the first initiation with the upward pointing triangle given at the third. It also incorporates the individual symbols used to represent the elements of Earth, Air, Fire and Water. Thus it is a symbol of completeness.

The hexagram can be used to symbolise the connection with planets (Figure 11). The seven classical planets (including Sun and Moon) are arranged around the points, with the Sun in the centre shining through the centre of all of them.

The hexagram is incorporated into one's robes by tying the cords worn around one's waist with a reef knot (left over right then right over left).

▲ *Figure 11 – The Planets on the Hexagram*

Using the centre of the hexagram to draw a circle that touches each point, then using each point from which to draw a similar sized circle that passes through the hexagram's centre, you end up with a symbol known as the Seed of Life (Figure 12). This symbol has been found in use in ancient Egyptian temples and has been the basis of study by sacred geometrics in recent years. As the Hebrew race came out of Egypt it's possible that this is another sign that the hexagram's roots are actually much older.

▲ *Figure 12 – Using the hexagram as the basis for the Seed of Life*

THE ANKH

The Ankh (Figure 13) is a symbol that represents life and has its roots in the ancient Egyptian tradition. It would not tend to be used generally in a Celtic-inspired Wiccan path as it is not a symbol that is often used outside of the Egyptian tradition and was never part of the Celtic cultural heritage. However, there are many Wiccans who, for their own reasons, opt for an Egyptian-inspired Wiccan path or use the ankh in a more eclectic sense. It is entirely possible that those souls that have been incarnating for a long time will have been through incarnations that include both Celtic and Egyptian. There are certainly common roots and connections. For this reason it is possible that someone who is advancing quickly on the spiritual path in the current incarnation is doing so because of a depth of karma that makes this possible and would therefore find a deep attraction to symbols outside of their current body's cultural roots.

The Ankh uses elements of symbols common to many paths. It is made up from a circle, denoted by the loop at the top of the Ankh representing the soul or divine spirit, descending into the Tau (a form of cross) that represents matter. It is most likely to be the original use of a cross symbol that later got taken up in various ways by other spiritual traditions. It is a symbol of life, both the physical life and the eternal, and often worn as an amulet of protection.

The ankh is associated with Isis and Her consort Osiris. The loop at the top can be seen to represent the womb of the Goddess whilst the T shape underneath is a phallic symbol representing the God. It thereby represents the life-giving interaction between Goddess and God. The ankh is sometimes depicted in Egyptian paintings being held to the nose of the deceased by the gods to symbolise the giving back of life's breath in the otherworld. The ankh also resembles a key and thus symbolises the key to the secret of eternal life.

▲ *Figure 13 – The Ankh*

36

THE CELTIC CROSS

The Celtic (or Solar) Cross (Figure 14) is a symbol that includes an amazingly complex set of correspondences considering its simplicity. It is a symbol that was used by our Celtic ancestors but is, as with most of these symbols, also one that has its origins elsewhere and has been adopted by other cultures and traditions.

In its most simple form the Celtic Cross can be seen to represent the four elements with Spirit in its centre surrounded by the never ending Circle that binds it all together. The traditional and commonly used Circle casting method detailed in Wiccan Spirituality is based on this symbolism. In Celtic-inspired Wicca the elements are usually positioned with Earth in the North, Air in the East, Fire in the South and Water in the West (Figure 15). However, it should be borne in mind that some other traditions that use similar symbolism sometimes put the elements in different positions which can be quite disorientating if you have become used to this system. Wiccans in the southern hemisphere may understandably reverse the representation. A similar system is used by those following a Native American path and it is interesting how many similarities there are between the Celtic ways and that of the Native Americans.

The Celtic Cross also represents the Goddess and God and the all encompassing Divine Spirit. The horizontal line being passive and receptive can be seen as representing the Goddess, the vertical line being active can be seen to represent the God with the Circle representing the one Spirit. This symbolism, whilst used in Wicca and being a symbol

▲ *Figure 14 – The Celtic or Solar Cross*

▲ *Figure 15 – The Celtic Cross showing the positions of the elements commonly used in Wicca*

used by our Celtic pagan ancestors and adapted by the Christian Church, is also found in Eastern theosophy.

With reference to this Eastern theosophy we can find a useful analogy, using the Celtic Cross, for the formation of the Cosmos. If we begin with the circle ○ this represents the nothing (zero) that contained everything. From the heart of this great potential came the first stirrings of movement. This is represented by the circle with a dot at its centre ⊙. From these first stirrings the Goddess was born, the passive receptive form of matter ⊖ for without the Goddess to receive and to give form there can be nothing else. Finally the God added motion and activity to spread this matter throughout the Cosmos ☐ bringing fertility to every sector.

This analogy is echoed in the creation myth of Diana found in Charles Leyland's *Aradia: The Gospel of the Witches*. In that story Diana is the Goddess, the 'first created before all creation'. She is the supreme darkness from Whom was born light in the form of a God – Lucifer. Having created Lucifer from the darkness that was Herself, Diana sees the beauty of this active light and so begins a love chase. This love chase is the creative interaction between passive and active, Goddess and God. Diana, the Creatress, pursues her God to the physical plane. Here She tricks Lucifer into making love with Her and in doing so brings the divine darkness, the passive creative force, into physical manifestation as Aradia the Earthly reflection of Diana. In this story we see the analogy that explains why pagans tend to see Goddess and God in cosmic form and also in more Earth-bound form giving each form separate names whilst clearly understanding that they come from one divine source.

In many Wiccan ceremonies the Celtic Cross is drawn on the foreheads of the participants in a ritual as a consecration. The most appropriate way of drawing it, would therefore be to draw the horizontal line first saying: '*I consecrate you in the name of the Goddess...*' then the vertical name, saying, '*and the God...*', then finally draw the circle around the cross in a sunwise direction, saying, '*in this their Circle.*' It is intended to be a reminder of the nature of our Creators and as a blessing upon us their creation.

THE SCOURGE AND THE KISS

Two very important symbols used in Wicca, and two that are usually paired together, are the Scourge and the Kiss represented as symbols as in Figure 16 as well as by an actual scourge and physical kiss. They

▲ *Figure 16 – The Kiss (left) and the Scourge (right) representing Perfect Love and Perfect Trust*

represent the two passwords that Wiccans use to enter the Circle and the necessary attitude to maintain as a working witch of 'Perfect Love' (the Kiss) and 'Perfect Trust' (the Scourge).

Perfect love and perfect trust are more than just the attitudes that we require to work with others in a Circle. They represent the attitudes that we need to develop with the Goddess and God themselves. The significance of this may be immediately apparent, but the meaning becomes even more important as one develops towards the higher levels of consciousness. When one begins to question why there is so much suffering in the World, it is important to remind ourselves that the physical plane is only an illusion, only part of the greater reality, and that no matter what degree of suffering we witness, these are all but lessons from which we can learn and grow. We need to learn to fully Love and Trust the Goddess and God in these situations, so that we can appreciate that this suffering, in the end, is for the good of all.

The scourge is symbolic of the purity of mind, body and spirit that we should do our best to incorporate into ourselves at all levels as a priestess or priest in service to the gods. The scourge is often used as a tool within ritual to remind us of this necessity. Sadly, its association with modern sexual sadomasochism tends to confirm the misunderstanding of those new to or outside Craft circles, and for that reason many reject the scourge as a symbol. It is important, whether the scourge is used or not, that the principle it represents is not lost for it is central to the successful development of a High Priestess or High Priest.

THE FIVE-FOLD KISS

The 'perfect love and perfect trust' is sometimes symbolised in ritual situations combined with the five-fold kiss that also acts to purify, bless and honour the High Priestess and others in the fully cast Circle. This is usually first conducted by the High Priest for the High Priestess just before 'Drawing Down the Moon' as well during initiation ceremonies on the initiate.

The High Priestess stands before the High Priest who is kneeling with head bowed to honour her. Initially she stands in the God position, feet together with arms crossed over her breasts, hands resting in front of her shoulders. He then kisses her feet and says: '*Blessed be your feet that have brought you to this place.*' He then kisses her knees and says: '*Blessed be your knees that shall kneel at the sacred altar.*' He then kisses her womb saying: '*Blessed be your womb that brings life.*' The High Priestess then moves to stand in the Goddess position, legs apart with arms outstretched towards the sky. The High Priest continues by kissing her breasts saying: '*Blessed be your breasts, formed in beauty*', and finally her lips, saying: '*Blessed be your lips that shall utter the sacred words.*'

When performed properly this is a most beautiful and loving part of the ritual. It should also be pointed out that one of the purposes of this is to raise the energy from below into the Priestess. The Priest, representing the force of the God, is lending his energy and invoking it into the Priestess. The feet correspond with the Earth energy that is then raised up the legs to the womb. The womb does not only actually bring life in many circumstances, it is also the region on the body that corresponds with the sacral energy centre which is the creative energy centre. The ritual then continues to raise the energy from this creative energy centre to the heart centre (between the breasts) then to the throat centre where this energy manifests in a higher form (just below the lips).

THE VESICA PISCIS

The Vesica Piscis (Figure 17) consists of two interlocking circles in which the circumference of each passes through the central point of the other. It is a symbol of great antiquity and has many interpretations based around a common theme within several paths.

To a Christian the Vesica Piscis is the root form of the Piscean fish symbol used by many – taken from the central part of the symbol. It is a badge displayed by followers of the Christian Jesus Christ – the Fisher King. It denotes the followers as fellow 'fisher of men' that has dominated throughout the Age of Pisces that is just ending.

To a Theosophist, the Vesica Piscis represents the Ring of the Cosmos and the Ring of Chaos. It thus represents the great duality in

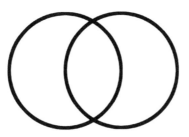

▲ *Figure 17 – The Vesica Piscis*

the cosmos, the creative force and the creative form, negative and positive, passive and receptive...good and evil even. This is the same duality that Wiccans perceive though using different terminology.

To a Wiccan, the Vesica Piscis can represent Goddess and God and the sexual creative energy they form to produce form through the central vulva section of the symbol. This then represents the creativity in the duality between feminine and masculine, black and white, negative and positive, form and force. The Vesica Piscis therefore makes an ideal symbol to utilise during a Wiccan handfasting where the male and female in the ceremony are joined as representations of the union between God and Goddess to work together in harmony as partners. Using this symbol helps to highlight the important balance and interdependence between masculine and feminine, and thus a 'marriage', that is at the heart of Wicca.

The symbol represents the way energies are brought together to create swirling vortices of energy in transformation at all levels from the sub-molecular to the cosmic.

In Glastonbury, the Vesica Piscis is a symbol that has been adopted by many elements within the broad community of new age incomers who occupy the area at the time of writing (including the author). It is a symbol that has been associated with Glastonbury, it would appear, for many centuries. Here too the symbol represents the dual energies (often) of Goddess and God, sometimes just of the Goddess, though the symbol found here has an added element. It has a sword piercing through the centres of the vesica binding the symbol together. This is the sword of St Michael, the serpent slayer. The tower that survives on top of Glastonbury Tor is also dedicated to St Michael and (in this author's opinion) stands to bind and restrict the feminine elements of the Goddess and thus restrict the energies under which paganism flourishes. The sword of St Michael needs to be removed in order for the energies to flow properly.

▲ *Figure 18 – The Vesica Pool in Chalice Well Gardens, Glastonbury*

There is one very important place in Glastonbury where the symbol of the sword has been removed (or at least removed from its position binding the two circles) from the Vesica. This is in the area known as Arthur's Court in the beautiful and lovingly cared-for Chalice Well Gardens at the foot of the Tor. Chalice Well (Figure 18) is a wonderful sacred garden open to the public, where all faiths are welcome and meditation encouraged. It has the well in which the famous red spring rises. The water is heavily loaded with iron, hence the metallic taste and the bright red residue the water leaves in the form of silt. The water is pumped from the well into a stream that runs through the gardens, past a couple of 'holy thorns' and several wonderful yew trees. Before entering the vesica-shaped pool at the bottom of the garden it goes through a walled

▲ *Figure 19 – The Vesica symbol as it appears above the entrance to Arthur's Court in Chalice Well Gardens, Glastonbury (with the sword removed). This area is where Glastonbury's powerful red and white springs cross, as do the masculine and feminine ley lines*

section known as Arthur's Court. Under a yew tree is a stone bench where one can sit and enjoy the sound of water splashing down a short waterfall in front of where you are sitting (an excellent place for cleansing crystal). This is the point where two great ley lines (known as the Michael and Mary lines) cross and is also where, underground, the red spring meets the white spring water. (The white spring water comes from inside the Tor and is loaded with calcium.) Above the door to this magical place is a vesica piscis symbol (Figure 19) showing the sword removed from its normal position. Sitting on this bench and closing ones eyes, it is easy even for the beginner to dive into a very deep meditation. It is very much a gateway to what some would call the Celtic Underworld – or Annwn. But then, this is an attribute that has been used for centuries for Glastonbury Tor known to many locals as Avalon.

EXERCISE – THE VESICA PISCIS

For this exercise you will need to find a pond or a lake where the waters are reasonably still. Choose a day when it isn't very windy so that the surface of the water isn't disturbed. Pick up two small stones that are about the same size and reasonably spherical in shape.

Stand at the water's edge holding a stone in each hand. Then throw the stones up so that they land in the water at the same time about five or six feet apart and watch the ripples they cause, and how these ripples interact with each other.

You should see, at first, a vesica pisces form, and as the ripples interact with each other and ripple out together across the pond, the two circular ripples of energy gradually blend together to form just one ring. This is symbolic of the way the Goddess and God energies work.

TALISMANS, AMULETS AND SEALS

Talismans are items that we have constructed and keep close to us that help to bring about either changes that we are in the process of invoking through an act of magic or simply for good luck. They can take many forms.

An amulet is usually an item worn for protection, when the need for protection is truly felt, or worn to bring a little extra energy during times of need. It is worth noting here that the need for protection is often exaggerated. As many of us have been brought up in cultures that are based on fears, whether from the dominant religion, through politics, or through the media, it is easy to understand how a certain paranoia filters into our psyche. In reality, if you approach life with love in your heart then there is rarely any need to fear anything – though there can be occasions when it is useful to guard yourself against negative energies coming from those around you. Crystals worn around the neck on a chain or a leather thong could be classed as an amulet. By picking an appropriate crystal you can use this to help calm nerves during a test or examination, bring a little extra strength when tired or recovering from an illness, etc.

Seals have been used through the ages as items used to invoke energies. One of the earliest known seals used is based around the pentacle, though many other symbols, many far more complex, have been used too. Seals can be drawn on paper or onto small wax tablets and used during magic ritual and then kept somewhere safe (such as on the altar) or carried around. A seal can basically incorporate any number of symbols appropriate to the work in hand. The choice of symbols needs to be ultimately down to the person or persons working the magic and be fully understood by them. A good symbol to use that may well appeal to many Wiccans is the Celestial Pentacle.

▲ *Figure 20 – Example of a Seal calling for peace and harmony*

Having cast a Circle, the appropriate gods, goddesses, guides and elementals are called upon to help with the work in hand. Making sure that every stroke is done with the intent of the ritual working in mind, the Pentacle is then drawn with other appropriate symbols incorporated within. Finally an appropriate wording is placed between the two outer rings to bind the spell.

The following seal (Figure 20) is just an example. The two symbols within the Pentacle represent the names of a High Priest and High Priestess (in ogham runes) who work as partners. The ritual intended to call for peace and harmony in their hectic lives, so the wording around the outside simply calls on the Goddess and God to work through them to attain this. The five other runes are examples of Futhark runes and is a symbol of protection. Being a Pentacle, the seal automatically incorporates the five elements (which were also called upon for assistance within the ritual Circle). In addition colours of an appropriate hue can add further meaning. For peace and harmony one might use pink, though you could also use colours representing the five elements. The important thing is to use what feels right for you, use symbols that have meaning for you, and to fill the ritual with rightful intent and feeling.

This is, of course, only one example of a seal. Other seals and talismans can be devised using all sorts of symbols as deemed right and appropriate to the witch whilst bearing in mind, as in everything we do, the ethical basis and the three-fold law. The planetary tablets shown in detail in Chapter 8 on Planetary and Zodiacal influences can be utilised if a certain planetary energy is deemed appropriate to the work in hand, for instance, as can any of the other symbols detailed in this book.

5

THE SEVEN PLANES

Seven is a number that comes up a lot in all sorts of things, but especially in spiritual models used throughout many cultures. In this volume we will be looking at the seven planes of reality, the seven energy centres, the seven colours of the rainbow, the seven Circles of Annwn, the seven paths on a spiral maze, and will be touching upon the seven rays of energy that penetrate all things and affect us on all levels. There are many other examples from all sorts of different traditions such as the seven notes in a musical scale, seventh heaven, the seven virtues and the seven deadly sins, the dance of the seven veils (an erotic dance that has strong spiritual roots), the seven keys to the mystery tongue, and in the Christian Bible (Revelations) the seven seals, seven angels with seven trumpets, seven stars, seven churches in Asia, seven spirits before the throne, etc. It is useful to explore some of these models for several reasons. Firstly, there is a great truth behind most of these teachings that transcends any particular spiritual path or cultural belief system. Secondly, when we begin to look beyond the surface of the gloss of the myths, teachings and systems of our own culture and do the same with others, we readily begin to see remarkable similarities that clearly have their origins at a common source. That is not to suggest that those cultural glosses are not of value: they most certainly are in my opinion. But it is also my opinion that to understand where other cultures are coming from (and to recognise that beneath the façade it is the same place) we can begin to understand that where we are heading is the same place even if we have necessarily taken different routes. Something that I always emphasise to my students is that there are no right ways or wrong ways, just different ways.

It is easy to understand how our ancestors would have viewed a rainbow as a glorious message from the divine. The fact that it was nearly always followed by a bout of bright sunshine added weight to the beneficence of the miraculous message in the sky. Many of us today feel nature tugging at our heart strings when we witness the breath-taking beauty of a rainbow. Its message is one of the biggest and most perfect clues to the path of spiritual enlightenment anywhere to be found.

What do you see when you look at a rainbow? The answer to that question may depend on the individual type of mind viewing it. However, the number and colours associated with the rainbow are synonymous with the seven planes that we discover on our journey of spiritual development. The colours match up with the seven planes of reality that go under various names depending on the religious culture. They are visible representations associated and linked to the seven energy rays that match up with and work through the seven main 'chakra' energy centres within the body.

It should also be borne in mind that the seven colours of the rainbow consist of the three primary colours of red, yellow and blue and four secondary colours that can be created from a combination of the three. It is worth spending some time meditating on the significance of this. The pagan Goddess often comes in triple form which matches up to the three primary colours. Red is closest to the spiritual plane representing the passion of spiritual fire; yellow is associated with the mental plane; blue with the emotional plane; and to make green, associated with earth and the physical plane, one needs to combine yellow and blue – mental and emotional energy.

Instead of the Hindu word 'chakra' for the whirling energy centres throughout the body I prefer to use the term 'energy centres'. Any term is more meaningful if it is in a language you understand. There are many energy centres throughout the body. They are the unseen energy lines that network the etheric body of a person, or any object containing living spirit, with everything else. These energy lines, like the central nervous system to which they are closely linked, criss-cross the etheric outer layer of the physical form. They act as the interface between the physical and the other planes that our energies penetrate. Where the most lines cross are what are known as the major energy centres (generally seven in total). There are also many lesser and minor energy centres that are also vital. The seven major energy centres are tuned in, much like a radio, each to a certain vibrating frequency that penetrates the planes. They also link in to and align themselves with seven glands through the body. Table 2 shows how each of these major energy centres corresponds with a colour of the rainbow, a plane of reality, a spiritual kingdom and a physical gland in the body. It is through these vibrating frequencies that 'messages' are passed from the spiritual plane, the realm

Table 2 – Correspondences of the major energy centres

Colour	Energy centre	Spiritual kingdom	Plane of reality	Gland
Red	Base of spine	Mineral	Physical	Adrenals
Orange	Sacral	Human	Lower emotional	Gonads
Yellow	Solar plexus	Animal	Higher emotional	Pancreas
Green	Heart	Vegetable	Lower mental	Thymus
Light blue	Throat	Soul	Higher mental	Thyroid
Indigo	Third Eye	Planetary	Lower Spiritual	Pituitary
Violet	Crown	Cosmic	Higher spiritual	Pineal

of the goddesses and gods, through the mental and emotional planes to the physical and back again – not unlike a radio wave. To become one with the goddess and gods we need to train our 'apparatus' to translate these messages more clearly.

Figure 21 shows the positions of the seven major energy centres and twenty-one lesser centres. The twenty-one lesser energy centres are:

- Two in front of the ears where the jaw bones connect.
- One behind each eye.
- One above each breast.
- One at the top of the breast bone close to the thyroid gland.
- One in each palm of the hand.
- One in each sole of the foot.
- One near the liver.
- One connected with the stomach (related to the solar plexus major centre).
- Two connected to the spleen that work together as one.
- One at the back of each knee.
- One (particularly powerful one) at the back of the head connected with the vagus nerve.[1]
- One close to the solar plexus.
- One connected to each of the gonads.

The centres aligned to the palms of the hands can be and often are utilised in healing work.

---

[1] This energy centre is sometimes referred to as a major centre. It is a very important centre that corresponds with Daat – the hidden knowledge – on the Tree of Life.

✻ MAJOR
✳ LESSER

▲ *Figure 21 – Major and lesser energy centres within the etheric part of the physical body*

There are also forty-nine smaller centres – or minor centres. These include points aligned with the fingers and toes, the heel, wrists, etc.

A thorough study of the major and lesser energy centres is a useful exercise. Such an understanding in itself helps development by offering an explanation for energies experienced during your work. This understanding is particularly useful if, as many Wiccans do, you undertake a lot of healing work. However, it should be borne in mind that concentrating on any particular centre in an effort to develop one particular area is highly inadvisable. Forcing the development of an individual centre through breathing or any other method risks creating a serious imbalance that can cause dire consequences. This is an error quite commonplace in many esoteric paths and one to look out for in others. It is important that all the centres are allowed to develop at a pace determined and controlled by the Higher Self and the guides with which we work, rather than to subject that development to conscious control driven by an impatient desire for progress.

If a student were to concentrate on a consciously forced development of the third eye or crown centre, for instance, it is quite likely that person's energy would create an imbalance with the other centres causing grounding problems. The student may well find that extra-sensory functions would develop, but at the cost of losing touch with the emotional and physical centres. The consequences of such development are sadly commonplace and can be quite distressing and ugly.

Remember (and trust) that at all times development in a student of pure motive and reasonable discipline is assured simply by a combination of study and practice. This is true even if the speed of development does not match the rate of desire. Patience is a lesson that needs to be thoroughly appreciated. It is quite normal for development to come in spurts as opposed to a smooth transition. The body's energy centres grow in activity, often at quite a rapid pace; this is usually then followed by a period of adjustment that allows for the physical body and its conscious control to get used to the new energies and learn how to use them. Once the physical has got used to the energies then a further spurt of development tends to follow when it is ready. The conscious mind is often astounded and impressed by the apparently new abilities the development makes possible and wants to experience more. This is the danger point that needs to be recognised and avoided. If you force the development at a pace that is too fast for the conscious mind to keep up with, then you would be opening yourself up to the possibility of a whole range of potential psychological dysfunctions. Allow the energies to set their own pace and learn to go with the flow. You can safely help things along by a strict discipline of meditation backed up with plenty of academic study and practical exercises.

THE CELTIC VIEW OF THE SEVEN PLANES

So far we have looked at the seven planes as symbolised by the rainbow and the seven energy centres that many who have studied 'new age' thought, Theology, or Eastern spiritual practice will be familiar. But what has it got to do with witchcraft, especially a Celtic-inspired form of witchcraft?

Well, at the beginning of this chapter I said that 'there is a great truth behind most of these teachings that transcends any particular spiritual path or cultural belief system.' This is particularly true of the eastern system of the seven chakras. Witches, whether Wiccan or otherwise, work with energies and, whether the practitioner is fully aware of it or not, the energy tends to flow through these centres in various ways.

As for the connection with the seven planes in the Celtic belief system, that is a slightly longer story.

One of the most compelling myths in the Celtic lands is that of King Arthur. The stories with which most of us are perhaps most familiar have been heavily rewritten and Christianised. The original myths provide a great deal of teaching that is largely lost in the rewriting. In the Christianised version, Arthur sends his knights off on quests to find the 'holy grail' – the search every corner of the physical Earth without success until one learns to look where nobody else had. However, in the earlier pagan versions we find that the holy grail is in fact Cerridwen's cauldron. The cauldron is to be found in Annwn at Caer Sidi (the Castle of Glass). Annwn one of the names for the Celtic 'otherworld' or the centre of the Celtic spiritual world. Caer Sidi is one of seven castles whose gates one needs to gain entrance in order to find the cauldron. Annwn is separated from the world of form, the physical plane, by seven concentric circles known as the Circles of Annwn (Figure 22). The 'circles' are separated by stretches of water that one needs to cross in order to reach each of the castles (and thus their gates) on your journey to the centre.

The castles that one passes on the way are: Caer Ochren, Caer Fandy-Manddwy, Caer Goludd, Caer Rigor, Caer Feddwyd, and Caer Pedryfan – ending eventually at Caer Sidi.

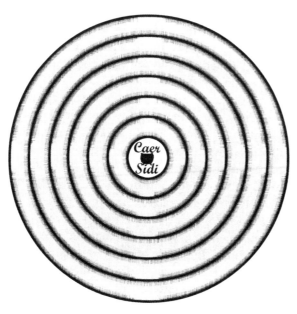

▲ *Figure 22 – The Circles of Annwn*

▲ *Figure 23 – The spiral labyrinth*

This is quite just another way of representing the seven planes and one which our Celtic ancestors developed in tune with their own cultural terms from an understanding that somehow transcended all cultures. At the beginning of this chapter I stated that 'when we begin to look beyond the surface of the gloss of the myths, teachings and systems of our own culture and do the same with others, we readily begin to see remarkable similarities that clearly have their origins at a common source'. The example above shows the Celtic connection with the seven planes. In the East there is a cosmological model that is almost identical to that of the Celts. In this system there are seven islands or continents called 'Dwipas' which form concentric rings, separated by the ocean, that surround a place called 'Jambu Dvipa' at its centre. This model is also almost identical to one found in the Iranian culture, although the 'Dwipas' are instead called 'Karshvars' and the temple at the centre is called 'Karshvar Qaniratha'.

I'm sure there are many amongst the human race who would go to war over such differences as to whether the spiritual centre should be called Annwn, Jambu Dvipa, Karshvar Qaniratha, or Heaven, but would we really be fighting over models that are actually divided by little more than different names!

Another wonderful model, and one that is found throughout many parts of the world, is the spiral maze, sometimes called the Cretan Maze. This is shown in Figure 23. This has been found carved into rock in places far apart at a time when it is presumed that there was little chance of meeting and communicating such ideas. One very good example can be found in a little valley between Tintagel and Boscastle in Cornwall. A very large example, in elongated form, can be found around the Tor at Glastonbury (Figure 24). (Though it must be pointed out that this was popularised by the authoress Dion Fortune – may the Goddess

▲ *Figure 24 – Glastonbury Tor – the rings form a labyrinth with seven levels*

bless her – and the rings may possibly have been ancient levels carved out for planting crops that just coincidentally match a labyrinth pattern. Not that such an idea should stop you walking the Tor if you get the chance, for the energies in Avalon are exceptional and the area has been a spiritual centre for thousands of years, long before the Christians built their first church in Britain there.) It is no accident that the Tor has been associated itself with the myth of Gwynn Ap Nudd, a Celtic God who guards the entrance to Annwn.

One of the great tragedies of Celtic mythology is that there are no intact surviving records of some of its older teachings. They spent many years being handed down by word of mouth, any then became mixed and overlaid with Christian interpretations, with historic events, and with added reinterpretations following the influences of invading cultures such as the Saxons and Normans. There are a number of dedicated modern historians who are valiantly doing there best to strip away all these degrading overlays, but a great deal has been lost. One good example that, when one strips away the historic records that have slipped in, gives another clue that the Celts had an esoteric understanding of the seven planes and the energies of the Watchers that work through them is in a poem attributed to Taliesin. It takes the form of a dialogue between Taliesin and Merlin. The relevant section reads:

> *'Taliesin:*
> *The seven sons of Elifer, seven heroes,*
> *Will fail to avoid seven spears in the battle.*
>
> *Merlin:*
> *Seven fires, seven armies,*
> *Cynfelyn in every seventh place.*
>
> *Taliesin:*
> *Seven spears, seven rivers of blood,*
> *From seven chieftains fallen.*
>
> *Merlin:*
> *Seven score heroes, maddened by battle,*
> *To the forest of Celyddon they fled.*
> *Since I, Merlin, am second only to Taliesin,*
> *Let my words be heard as truth.'*

The references to Elifer, Cynfelyn and Celydden[2] are historic overlays, or perhaps added analogies that had greater meaning at the time, but reading around these we do get a model of the energies, driven by a hierarchy of forces, that work through the seven planes.

'I AM A STAG OF SEVEN TINES'

The 'stag of seven tines' is an image of the Horned God that makes an appearance in the mythological poetry of the bard Taliesin. Besides being an image of what is certainly one of the oldest pagan deities it is also one quite appropriate to use as a visualisation when working with the energies of the seven planes.

A stag of seven tines is one that has well developed antlers that have seven points on each side, so fourteen in all. This can be used to visualise the energy from the seven planes, both the positive and negative elements. As the antlers are attached to the head we can see this as the energies entering into the mind through which we achieve balance not just between the seven planes, but between the positive and negative

---

[2] Elifer is a northern chieftain. The battle (of Arderydd in Cumbria) was between his sons and Gwenddolan in 573 CE. Cynfelyn (also known as Cunobelin or Shakespeare's Cymbeline) was King of the Trinovantes tribe, one of the most powerful kings in pre-Roman Britain – i.e. not contemporary with Elifer. Celyddon is the Welsh name for a tribe of Picts, possibly the Dalradians, who ruled the Border and southern Scottish region. Coed Celyddon was the name of a forest in the central Border area of Britain.

elements of each. The stag is a beautiful and noble creature, by working with this image you too can take on these attributes.

THE SEVEN RAYS

The Seven Rays are the energies that flow through the seven planes. Theosophists such as Helena Blavatsky, Alice Bailey, Dion Fortune and others, have written some excellent theses on these Seven Rays which are worth studying and getting to understand in great detail (Alice Bailey's work with a highly developed Tibetan spiritual guide runs to many volumes and thousands of pages).

The Rays can be considered to be energies, each with a different attribute which together make a whole, just as with the light you can observe as a rainbow. In fact the visible light is part of this whole system of energy flow, and therefore the rainbow colours do form an actual part of these seven ray energies, but only the visible part is a tiny fraction of the total reality.

Being an indivisible part of the whole, each of our souls is primarily influenced by just one of these rays. In other words, each soul will specialise, though all the rays flow through every part of our whole. It is therefore possible, with work, to determine what soul type you are by working out which ray dominates at that level. Bear in mind though that just as the soul specialises by working predominantly with a particular ray, our emotional and physical bodies also choose to work primarily with a particular ray, and different ones through different incarnations. This helps to get a broad range of experiences.

There are a great many ways of describing the influences these rays provide. They are described in the works of Alice Bailey as follows:

- 1st Ray – The Ray of Power, Will and Purpose
- 2nd Ray – The Ray of Love – Wisdom
- 3rd Ray – The Ray of Active Creative Intelligence
- 4th Ray – The Ray of Harmony through Conflict
- 5th Ray – The Ray of Concrete Science or Knowledge
- 6th Ray – The Ray of Idealism or Devotion
- 7th Ray – The Ray of Order or Ceremonial Magic

It is worth bearing in mind that a soul can be influenced primarily by any one of these rays, whilst a physical incarnation (at this time) is usually associated with one of the lower four. The rays affect us by working through the etheric interface, each one primarily working through one of the seven energy centres, though each energy centre receives the force of each ray attribute through fractions or sub-rays of the totality directed towards us.

Because these rays represent the energy flowing through the totality of existence they also affect everything from the cosmic to the micro-cosmic. Each age is affected by a different ray, each planet is affected by a different ray (and the energy flows through them to us), each nation and culture is also affected by a different ray. It is largely through this process that life is able to gain experience (karma) in all its range of possibilities. The Piscean Age, for instance, is affected primarily by the 6th Ray (of Idealism and Devotion) whilst the energies of the coming Aquarian Age are already being felt which are dominated by the 7th Ray (of Order and Ceremonial Magic).

A fuller explanation of the metaphysical ways the Rays work from the perspective of a Wiccan will appear in a future volume, but it should be noted that a thorough study would require several volumes, dedicated to it. This simplistic explanation, I hope, will suffice for the purposes of introduction along with further references in this current volume.

PHYSICAL PLANE

The physical plane is the one with which we are all most familiar during the time we spend incarnate. It can be quite unsettling at first to discover that this plane is but a fraction of reality and this realisation is, perhaps, the first step in any process of spiritual development. The physical plane is one of a set of energy fields vibrating at a range of frequencies. When we leave the spiritual plane at the other end of the spectrum, we require time to settle ourselves. The gap between the physical and the spiritual is one that we eventually begin to close down as we grow with experience through a number of incarnations. We begin to realise, at a certain stage of development, that there are things beyond that which we commonly experience in the physical, and that it is as real as anything else, not just a figment of an overactive imagination, but a reality.

We come to this realisation in lots of different ways.

Each of the planes has a set of seven sub-planes. The physical plane is no exception. Even without any esoteric training, we are readily aware of the first three sub-planes on the physical – solid, liquid and gas (each gradually less dense than the previous). Also part of the physical are four etheric levels, also gradually less dense than the one before. The etheric part of the physical plane acts as the interface with the rest of our bodies (again each one is less dense than the previous).

The etheric body is quite easily seen as a kind of energy shadow around the solid physical body (and around other living things such as plants and trees). It extends only a short distance around the body and has a reasonably well-defined outline. Some people confuse this with the aura which belongs to the astral body rather than the physical and extends beyond the etheric.

EXERCISE – SEEING THE ETHERIC BODY

This exercise works best if the room you are in is not too bright. It also helps if you hold your hands up so that there is a plain background behind them. Patterned backgrounds act as a camouflage.

Hold one hand up about 18 inches to 2 feet in front of your eyes and bring your forefinger towards your thumb so that they are nearly touching. Allow the focus of your eyes to soften just a little and you will see what looks like a faint band, or shadow, of light stretching between the finger and thumb.

Now try pulling the finger away from the thumb a little and you will see this band of light stretch and then separate like a piece of elastic. This is the outline of the etheric body. Unlike the aura it never separates from the physical body as it is part of it.

You can also look for this shadow around other living things such as plants or trees.

If you have a partner who is willing to help you, ask them to stand in the room against a plain background and look for the etheric body around them by softening the focus of your eyes in the same way. Notice how it shows up around areas that are free of clothing. By asking them to remove some more of their clothing you will get an idea of how clothing interferes with the etheric energy. This is one of the reasons why many witches work 'skyclad' (i.e. naked).

DIET

'You are what you eat!' In esoteric terms this is not entirely true, but your physical body certainly consists of what we take into our bodies and that has a profound effect on how we function and therefore how we are able to perceive reality. In reality our physical bodies are a temporary form that we have adopted – you are in actuality something very different, or at least a lot more, behind the veils of illusion. This, however, doesn't mean that we should reject our physical form, far from it, though many will be incarnating to learn this lesson. By the time we have properly opened ourselves to be one with the Goddess and God then we need to have learned to treat the physical form with the respect it deserves.

Your diet is a very important consideration in development for many reasons. If your physical body isn't functioning well then the etheric interface with the other planes is not going to function well either. Our physical body is largely dependent on what we take into our mouth and digest in our stomach. This heavily influences our mechanical functions, our brain's function and all the other functions from the obvious to the most subtle. We absorb into our systems fat, fibre, vitamins, minerals, etc. But we also absorb into our bodies the energies of the food, some of its life spirit.

The eating of meat is of vital consideration. Putting aside the ethical considerations for a moment, we should consider how well our body is going to function by absorbing dead and rotting flesh. The life-force (especially in the case of meat that has been frozen or preserved another way for a considerable time) has largely dissipated. The animal almost certainly died, even in the most humane of abattoirs, in shock having lived a life of boredom and misery. Are these the sort of energies that are going to be healthy to absorb? Our bodies have developed to be omnivorous – we can live on meat and/or vegetable and thus have a choice. However, our systems are not ideally designed for digesting large quantities of meat; at best it can cope well with meat in relatively small quantities. The energy we need through eating is derived from a plant, so consuming that energy second-hand via an animal is not exactly efficient. Despite this, many people insist on eating relatively huge quantities of flesh as if it was the most important source of nutrition which is far from the case. It generally consists of high levels of fat and fibre of a nature that is difficult to digest. In many modern cases it also consists of high levels of hormones that can remain active after absorption into our bodies and generate abnormal growth patterns. Many forms of cancer are attributable to high levels of meat intake, not to mention diseases such as BSE that currently remain dormant in many individuals. A meat-eater will find that the slow processing of flesh within the body, and all the fatty residues left behind, tend to make the body slow and stodgy. This in turn makes the way the brain functions rather slow and inefficient. This will not be fully realised until a vegetarian diet is adopted. One of the first things that new vegetarians experience is an amazing vitality. They find they feel full of energy, they feel light and bouncy and they tend to find their brains work with far more clarity.

Having said all of that, if you feel the compulsion to eat meat then it would be wise not to resist. Eating meat is often associated with a need to deal with issues on a karmic level. There are better ways to deal with karmic issues, but for some of us this is the only way. It is wise, however, to at least recognise this.

The traditional British meal of 'meat and two veg' has got to be one of the most boring on this planet. If you suggest to somebody used to such a diet that they try vegetarianism then the first thing they imagine is their dinner plate with the meat removed, leaving nothing but two piles of rather bland boiled vegetables. In that situation it is no wonder that they don't find the prospect attractive. However, a vegetarian diet isn't (or shouldn't be) like this at all. A good vegetarian diet consists of a whole range of foods that has fallen out of favour in the modern British diet and yet potentially opens up a whole new range of nutritious and flavoursome food.

A well-planned vegetarian diet can be the healthiest of all. There is nothing that our bodies require that cannot be obtained from vegetables. In fact, a vegan diet (one that denounces dairy products and eggs) can be the healthiest of all, as long as it is well thought through. It is no use though restricting a diet, vegetarian or otherwise, to fast foods that may have been highly processed and frozen. The processing and freezing may well save the food from rotting, but it destroys a great deal of life-force in the procedure.

The best foods to buy are fresh, local and seasonal. It is a useful habit to follow one's instincts as to the needs of the body. When picking foods, use your receiving hand and notice the reactions. Those foods that our body instinctively recognises as useful will make themselves known if you take notice of these reactions. There will be strong pull towards what you need and a repulsion against what you do not.

From a spiritual advancement point of view it is important to eat a well-balanced diet and to avoid gluttonous behaviour (though that is not to say that the occasional feast, especially when related to one of the pagan festivals, is not good for the spirit). The best foods to eat are fresh fruits and vegetables, nuts and grains. Organic food helps to avoid the many dubious chemicals that leave residues in our food. These chemicals are damaging to our physical bodies as well as the earth. Locally grown produce is particularly good for two reasons. Firstly, eating that which is seasonally available helps you to tune into the natural seasonal cycles; secondly it is more environmentally friendly as it hasn't required vast amounts of polluting fuel to transport it to you from far off places.

Taking on board plenty of liquid is also useful. Drinking several litres of good quality spring water every day helps to keep the whole system clear and vital. It helps to keep our internal organs working well, and if our physical organs are functioning at their prime then there is far more chance of their etheric elements working well and all that is connected to it. The most ideal source of water is a natural spring, and you are very lucky if you have a clean source near you from which you can draw it yourself. Avoid tap water. Tap water contains all sorts of damaging chemical additives (often including fluoride which is a waste by-product from heavy metal sources) and usually tastes quite foul. Spring water tends to retain its full life-force and helps to keep the whole system clear and functioning at peak efficiency. Whatever we eat, remember that our bodies are largely made of water and the quality of the water has a profound effect.

Following the seasonal tide of locally available fruit and vegetables helps you to tune in to nature's cycles as well as helping to ensure you get the freshest available. It also helps to support the local economy (especially if not bought from a supermarket chain). Even better, is to grow at least some of the food yourself if you have the facilities. Working with the soil, learning how to nurture the plant as it grows, is another very good way of learning about nature – working directly with Her energies – and ensuring you know exactly what has gone into the food.

A BLESSING FOR FOOD

Here are three examples for blessings that can be used before any meal. It is useful to get into the habit of doing this. First of all it gives thanks for what we have received, secondly it honours the Goddess and God for the energy they put into it. After I have said such words, either out loud or privately, I tend to look at what I have on my plate and briefly visualise the raw ingredients growing in the fields. I find this helps to build a connection with the spirits that have gone into its production.

> *'Each meal beneath this roof,*
> *Will be mixed together in the names of the Goddess,*
> *Who gave them growth.*
> *Milk and eggs and butter,*
> *The good produce of our flock.*
> *There shall be no disharmony in our land,*
> *Nor in our dwelling,*
> *In the name of the God,*
> *Who bequeathed to us the power,*
> *With the blessing of the Sun.*
> *Humble us at thy altar,*

By thy sanctuary around us.
Consecrate the produce of our land,
Bestow prosperity and peace,
In the names of the Goddess and God.
So must it be.'

'*Lady and Lord, Goddess and God,*
I give humble thanks for the food that you have provided,
May it nourish my body to aid me in my work,
In your service.
Blessed be.'

'*Gracious Mother,*
Darksome and Divine,
Bless my food,
Bless my wine.
Give me Health, Wealth and Wisdom,
The Divine Three,
And as I will,
So mote it be!'

EXERCISE – PHYSICAL NEEDS

This exercise should be carried out when you have a few quiet hours to yourself, initially around the time of the full moon.

Unplug your phone, turn off any mobile phones and do everything you can to ensure you are not going to be disturbed. If you share your home with other people then ask them to respect that you would like just a few hours without being disturbed to do something for yourself.

Run yourself a nice hot bath. (If you only have a shower then that will have to do, but a bath is much better for this.) Place a number of candles (preferably green ones) around the bath room and light something earthy incense – sandalwood would be a good one for this.

Put a few drops of an appropriately earthy essential oil in the bath or make yourself a herb pouch (see below). Also prepare some light massage oil and put just a few drops of the same oil into the massage base. Light the candles and incense and turn the lights off. Close the bathroom door. Say out loud: 'This is a time just for me and I will not be disturbed for anything.'

Strip off all your clothes and remove any jewellery.

Take the massage oil and rub it into your body. Ensure that you rub plenty into your neck and shoulders, around your chest and around your waist and buttocks then get into the hot bath.

Have a good long relaxing soak. You can always top the bath up with a little more hot water if it gets cold.

When you have finished, get out of the bath, take a towel and pat (rather than rub) yourself dry. (You do not want to rub off all the oil – it will soak in.)

Still naked, find somewhere warm to sit with your journal. If you are comfortable sitting crossed-legged on the floor (perhaps with a cushion under your backside) then do so, but sitting comfortably is the important thing as with any meditation.

On a fresh page in your journal write 'physical' at the top and under that write three headings – needs; wants; and not wanted.

Take your time and give each plenty of thought. When you have done so write down the things you consider to be your physical needs, wants and things you have that you would rather not. Remember, these are physical things – not emotional or other things.

When you feel you have completed this exercise, finish it with a short meditation, then put on some clean clothes.

Periodically throughout the month, after a meditation, review this list and see if you can cross things off of the 'needs' list. If you have things under the 'not wanted list' see if you can do something to get rid of them, preferably giving them away to someone who may have a better use for them, or to a charity shop.

Repeat this exercise when the moon is at Her darkest and compare lists.

EXERCISE – GROUNDING

Grounding is probably one of the most valuable and important exercises you will use throughout your work as a witch. It is best used both before and after any work. Many students, beginners and advanced alike, find that their work does not have the desired effect because of a lack of grounding.

If you do not feel fully grounded before you start any work and cannot get to the point where you feel thoroughly grounded, do not proceed!

Grounding, just as in an electrical circuit, ensures that any excess energy in you (or around you) is fully earthed. It ensures that any energy not intended for the work at hand is absorbed by the Earth Goddess both before the work (so that it doesn't affect that work), and after (so that it doesn't affect you unduly). If you feel stressed or light-headed to any degree then you are almost certainly not fully grounded. Get into the habit of always making a mental scan of how you feel before and after any work and take appropriate action.

There are many techniques used for grounding. Ensuring that you eat something like a dry biscuit with plenty of water is probably one of the easiest and best methods to start with. When you progress on to working full rituals in a fully cast Circle you will notice that many of the rituals end with what is known as the Ceremony of Cakes and Wine. This ceremony has spiritual significance, but it is also included at the end of a ritual to help the participants ground.

Other methods tend to involve some form of visualisation.

Stand with your feet firmly on the ground, your legs bent just a little at the knees so that you feel fully balanced. There should be no strain in the body. Close your eyes and work through your body from your head to your toes concentrating on each muscle in turn ensuring that it is soft and relaxed. When you get to the soles of your feet, visualise the excess energy following into the Earth. Ask (we make requests of the divine – we do not make orders!) the Goddess to deal with the energy and let it dissipate. Remember to thank the Goddess at the end by saying 'Blessed Be'.

The above exercise works well if you visualise yourself as a tree with roots going deep into the ground.

Another way of grounding, and a good one if you are working in a sitting position, is to put your palms on the ground and visualise the excess energy flowing into the ground through the centre of your palms.

Grounding can also be achieved by walking around slowly and placing the sole of your foot flat on the ground with each step whilst feeling for the Earth beneath. Any of the methods work best if you have bare feet. However, if you have become stressed (perhaps after a difficult meeting) it can work well if you take a slow walk around the block or through a park in your shoes – you can therefore do this without drawing attention to yourself.

Most people feel more relaxed after a peaceful walk in the countryside. Fresh air and being close to nature is always good for the spirit, and is a good grounding experience whether the person involved is consciously grounding or not. This can therefore be used to help others, even if they are not of an esoteric nature – just take them for a simple countryside walk or, better still, encourage them to go on their own.

These methods work by using lesser energy (or chakra) centres that exist within the soles of your feet and the centres of your palms.

If after doing a grounding exercise you still do not feel fully balanced then repeat the process. If you still do not feel grounded then it is best not to proceed with any elaborate work and going back to light meditations is the best advice.

There are various crystals that you can carry around with you to help you remain grounded. I have found that any form of jasper, or a green agate work well. Any iron-based crystal such as pyrite or hematite can work well, but they can sometimes be too strong – the grounding effect of these can become rather draining if you use them all the time. I have known people to wear hematite necklaces or bracelets on a regular basis and then wonder why they feel so tired all of the time. This is the powerful grounding effect of the crystal that is draining energy out of the system – sometimes useful in small bursts, but not always helpful.

LOWER EMOTIONAL PLANE

The lower emotional plane is also known as the lower astral plane. It is the plane that most of us know most vividly as the place in which we dream. It is a plane of fantasy, of illusion, of glamour, a plane where many on a spiritual path get totally lost, failing to see beyond the illusion – though it should be pointed out here that there are illusionary pitfalls to be overcome on all the planes. Because it is the first plane most people undertaking spiritual development discover beyond the physical, and because it is a world full of such fantasy and illusion, it is so very easy to fall into the trap of believing that enlightenment has been reached and that person begins to live the illusion as if it were the totality of reality. It is not. Bear this in mind or risk becoming lost in the illusion yourself! A study and understanding of Jungian psychology can help avoid many of these pitfalls.

It is necessary to work through the lower emotional plane. Just as with the other planes, it can't be side-stepped or avoided. In order to do so it is necessary to fully examine the lower self, the lower ego, in a totally honest and subjective fashion. The work requires you to look at yourself in the mirror and see all the bits that you like about yourself as well as all the bits that you dislike and learn to love yourself no matter what you see.

Emotions are an important element to our work as physical incarnation. Many would say that it is our ability to sense emotions that makes us human and that were we to lose that sense then we would stop being human, though we should eventually learn through our development that a degree of detachment is actually necessary. This is what makes working through the lower emotional plane so daunting and such a difficult step. Emotion is important, but we do need to become masters of our emotions so that we rule them rather than them ruling us. This does not mean that you will lose the ability to love, to care, even to get angry (for anger is just an emotion) but it does mean that you will learn how to take a stance beyond the emotions, when need arises, and see everything from a new a greater perspective. You will be able to love and care more deeply than ever – you can learn to feel without getting engrossed or overwhelmed.

EGO

The lower emotional plane is the place where our lower ego resides. The ego, as has been discussed in the chapter on Jungian psychology, has two elements to it. It is the personality that is the façade we dress ourselves up in and show to the world, but it also has a hidden side called the shadow self. The shadow self is one that we need to come to terms with before we can progress much further, otherwise it will create a blockage that will inevitably lead down any one of many dark and blind alleys. The personality is one that we have developed and adopted during the present incarnation. We develop it and dive into it and become it in order to undergo the karma (experience) that we have chosen from before we came into an incarnation. We can be so deeply involved in the personality aspect that we are totally unaware that there is anything beyond this. We can be totally unaware that the personality is only a part of the lower ego. The bits we don't like about the personality get buried and ignored in the shadow side of the lower ego and ignored because they are bits our conscious mind has decided it doesn't like, doesn't find attractive, and yet this doesn't mean they have been removed, doesn't mean they aren't there, and doesn't mean they don't affect us – they most definitely do. It is not until we confront these fragments we hide in the shadow and accept them as part of ourselves that we can honestly expect to grow beyond this plane. What's more, the longer we have spent burying things in the shadow and ignoring any confrontation, the more these fragments have linked together and built up complexes that further serve to create elaborate blockages and illusions. The longer we ignore them, the more elaborate the complexes become and the harder they are to unravel.

The personality is basically a mask that we wear. It is how we want people to see us. If we choose to undergo a process of spiritual development there is no reason why we cannot modify that mask so that gradually it begins to reflect the self in its higher manifestations. As confidence is gained, and as more is discovered about the self, the mask can gradually become more and more transparent until it essentially no longer exists and our higher selves shine through to the whole world with great clarity. By the time this point is reached, the energy flowing through all our bodies from all the planes becomes so unfettered that our aura glows brightly for all to witness.

OUR LADY THE MOON

In Wicca, one of the most important Goddess manifestations tends to be through the Moon. The Moon is closely associated with the lower emotional plane. There are many names associated with Her, and which ones you choose will depend on your own version of the path and your own tradition if indeed you choose to use names at all. More commonly She is recognised in Her triple aspects as mother, maiden and crone. The maiden is usually associated with the waxing Moon as it gets brighter from the new moon onwards, the mother is usually associated with the full Moon at the height of Her energy in Her full glory, and the crone is usually associated in Her waning aspect. Note the crone energy is associated with the deepest of wisdom and the inner knowledge, so the darkest element of the Moon's phase would be when we look within for that greatest of higher knowledge. You could rightly equate the maiden aspect with the ego's personality and the crone with the hidden shadow.

The time of the full Moon is a time when the connections with the other planes is so much easier to get a grip on. Ensuring that you use this time for meditation, contemplation and ritual, not only honours the Goddess but helps to open your energy centres to the flow of energy through which we tune in more clearly to the communication from beyond.

As Wiccans, and indeed all breeds of witches, tend to work with the Moon the monthly work in a Circle is important in the development. Regular work will not only strengthen the essential connection with the Goddess, but will gradually help the initiate to build strength on the lower emotional plane. Because the Moon is so closely associated with the emotional aspects of the self, this may offer a clue as to why far more women tend to be attracted to witchcraft than men. In very general terms, men tend to be far less willing to deal with their emotional aspects, far less willing to discover or admit to their feminine elements, and prefer not to go there, satisfying their lives with interests in the material world through sport or business. This is a great shame, though with the energies of the new age becoming felt by more and more, hopefully this situation will gradually change.

DREAMS

When we go to sleep we all enter the world of dreams. Even those who say they never dream do so; just because their conscious mind does not recall those dreams does not alter the fact that they do.

It is useful to keep your journal next to your bed so that you can make notes of any dreams that you do remember as soon as you awaken. You could keep a special journal for this purpose. If you do not write down notes about a dream you will often find that the details fade very quickly even though at the time of waking you are certain that you would remember everything. It tends to be the case that at a later time, when you are able to refer back to this journal, that the true meaning and value of those dreams becomes clear.

Remember that your subconscious tends to store and communicate ideas and messages in symbolic form rather than in words. This is true whether the source of any inspirational dreams comes from within (the Higher Self) or from an outside source (such as a spirit guide). If you are lucky then the occasional communication will come through in unmistakable and clear-cut words, but this is unfortunately rare – take special note when this happens as it will almost certainly be from a guide.

There are a great many books on the market that will help with dream analysis. Carl Jung undertook a lot of valuable work in this area and anything based on his work is worth obtaining. The symbols within dreams tend to be often, though not exclusively, based on archetypal concepts that come to us through the 'super-conscious' – that is they are common to all of us, no matter what our current range of experience and from a kind of 'central library' which all of us are able to tap into from the level of our Higher Self. This is not always the case, however, as certain life experiences can offer meanings different to those generally offered from the super-conscious level. The image of a fox would, for instance, be commonly interpreted as standing for great cunning, but if in the current life we had witnessed the barbarity of a fox hunt and seen a kill it could mean something entirely different.

It is also worth bearing in mind that characters that appear in our dreams may well look and sound like people we know – family, friends or other associates. A common mistake is to interpret such a dream as prophesying an incident or situation involving these people. More often, these characters represent aspects of ourselves – aspects that we have recognised as being represented by the main characteristics of those with whom we are familiar.

EXERCISE – MAKING A DARK MIRROR

'The mirror shows many things; things that were, things that are, and some things that have not yet come to pass.' – Spoken by Galadriel to Frodo, Lord of the Rings

There are many variations on the theme of dark mirrors. Many use a concave piece of glass, such as the front from a clock, for the purpose. Ready made concave mirrors can be bought, though I would advise against doing so for two reasons. Firstly, any tool will be of far greater use if you have put your own energy into making it. Secondly, a dark mirror is a highly personal item within the witch's armoury and only the user should ever look into it. If you have purchased a mirror then someone else's energy has gone into its manufacture and several people may have looked into it at the place of manufacture and whilst it was sitting in the shop.

A dark mirror is very easy and satisfying to make yourself. It doesn't need to be expensive. You don't need to use a concave piece of glass, a flat piece of glass works fine. If you do purchase one, then ensure that it is thoroughly cleansed before use and keep it somewhere safe from others.

Buy yourself a picture frame. It is best to buy a new one. An attractive frame makes it more pleasing to use, but this is a matter of preference and will not interfere much with the actual working of the mirror. In fact a frame that is too elaborate may cause an unhelpful distraction. You also need to buy a small pot of black enamel paint and a clear quartz crystal.

Carefully take the glass out of the frame and ensure it is thoroughly clean. Paint one side with the black enamel paint. If you accidentally get paint on the other side, don't worry as you can remove this with some white spirits later before it is thoroughly dried on. While the paint is drying, take the crystal, hold it in your hands for a few moments and concentrate on the purpose for which it is to be used (to aid in the work of uncovering your shadow self) and then smash it to pieces using a hammer. You will then have put plenty of your own energy into the fragments. These then need to be sprinkled as evenly as possible over the painted side of the glass while it is still drying.

The paint may take a good 24 hours to dry, so leave it somewhere safe overnight. When it is dry, put the glass back in the frame with the paint to the back. Remember to consecrate the tool, ideally at the time of a dark moon, before use.

'I consecrate this mirror for use in my work in the name of the Dark Goddess within. So must it be.'

EXERCISE – THE SHADOW SELF

During the phase of the dark Moon, just before the new Moon when She is entirely invisible, cast yourself as simple Circle on your own. You do not need an altar set up for this, but you will need your dark mirror and your journal or a note pad and pen.

Having cast the Circle, sit in the centre with your dark mirror propped up in front of you and two black candles burning just behind and on either side of the mirror. (If you cannot find black candles then another colour will do.) Allow yourself to clear your mind and settle down. Tune into the energy of the dark Moon as best you can. When you are settled, take some time to think about those people in your life who you dislike. They may, or may not, be people who you have fallen out with; they could be family members or even close friends that you occasionally fall out with. The important thing is, to write down everything about all these people that you either dislike, things that annoy you, habits that irritate you, etc. Be totally honest and thorough. Try not to express your thoughts in long sentences, but try to get the items down to as few words as possible – ideally just one word, such as 'selfish' or 'moody'.

When you have completed the list, cross out any names that you may have associated with the list and forgive yourself for having thought about them in a negative way if you feel the need.

Next, write your own name at the top of the page and being as objective as you possibly can, work down the list and tick which of these that you think others may at some time be possibly able to relate to you, at least from their perspective – put yourself in their shoes. If you are being totally honest you will almost certainly find that most of them do! The things we most dislike about others tend to be those things we have buried most deeply within our shadow self. Whilst we may deny them, this does not mean they are not there and that other people do not see them.

This does not mean these things are 'faults'. It does mean they are part of you and that as such you need to confront them and incorporate them into your whole self. Once you take charge of where these things come from, or what breeds those things, the seeds at the heart of the complexes, you can then accept them into your consciousness and let them dissolve gradually. Whilst we keep these things buried and refuse to deal with them, then they will continue to affect us from a level just behind our consciousness.

HIGHER EMOTIONAL PLANE

The higher emotional plane on the Tree of Life can be represented by two sephiroth; Netzach, meaning Victory and Hod, meaning Glory. It is the plane where we first begin to lift ourselves out of the everyday lower emotional energies and begin to feel an attachment to great things beyond ourselves. Here our connection is less with the lower self and more with those around us. Once developed further it can also be where we first begin to feel our attachment on a spiritual level to the Goddess and God.

There are many ways of connecting with the Goddess and God. They are after all at work all of the time in us and around us. We can witness and appreciate their work everywhere we look and to connect with them merely need to be and open ourselves up on this level to feel their presence within us. Regular walks in the countryside will aid this connection greatly, especially for those who live in a city or a large town. Whilst the beauty of the interaction between Goddess and God is evident in town, there is nothing like walking across open fields, or through wooded glades, to fully appreciate their full glory. Taking

▲ *Figure 25 – Spending time out at sacred sites is good for the Soul. The author at Boscowen Un Circle near Crows an Wra (Cross of the Witches) West Penwith, Cornwall*

time out from your busy routine to enjoy the wonders of nature will help you keep a healthy perspective on life and an understanding of the simple pleasures as well as to relieve the pent-up stress of modern life.

I have a very special place that I like to retreat to a few times a year. No matter what stresses I may have been under, the natural landscape of West Penwith in Cornwall (Figure 25) never fails to offer me a recharge. It is a place where the beauty of the Goddess and God shines through and has an energy that brings a peace to everyone. The people lucky enough to live there (and I intend to one day) have such a laid-back attitude to life. They don't earn a great deal of money, they don't appear to worry about it, they have a much stronger connection with the landscape and an appreciation of the simpler things in life than most living in the big towns and cities of the rest of the UK. O to sit on a Cornish cliff, with the waves crashing against the shore, watching the Sun set over the Scilly Isles and feeling the moon rise behind my neck while the breeze brushes gently against my cheek and the last few gulls make a last foray down below!

Such scenes make you realise that no amount of material wealth could ever satisfy you as much – who could want for more!

The higher emotional plane is where the connection with the divine entities is first felt and there is much that can be done to aid this process. Being out at special places is just one. Ensuring that you mark the Esbats and Sabbats is another. Bringing a few simple things into your everyday routine, such as meditation, helps enormously, and there are other things we can incorporate that are also useful. Beginning the day by making a small ritual out of opening your curtains and just taking in the light, and thanking the Lord and Lady for the opportunity another day affords is a good start. Taking a few moments at mid-day just to close your eyes and sense your connection with the Goddess and God helps too. This can help bring back some calm during a hectic work schedule and need only take a few minutes. Taking a few moments at sunset or at the end of the day in a similar way can also be very constructive and a useful habit to get into. You only need a few moments to yourself and there is no need to say anything out loud, it is just a private moment for yourself.

ASTRAL TRAVEL

Astral travel is something that many people begin to discover on this plane. It is possible to step out into the world of form by allowing the emotional body leave to venture forth on its own. You are in control at all times, of course, it is your emotional (or astral) body, so who else could be in control? To do this it is helpful to have become used to meditating and letting go of the conscious mind. Some practice in the art of visualisation is helpful as a starting point. Where you go is more than just a visualisation, but visualisation and the ability to hold such a visualisation, is the gateway.

It is possible to build a temple on the astral plane, in a place where nobody can interfere with it. You can make it as simple or as elaborate as you please. It can become your special place, somewhere to visit when-ever you want. Somewhere you can seek solitude and peace at any time. Such places need to be built on the higher levels of this plane as the higher levels exist outside the boundaries of what we tend to experi-ence as time and space, which is only an illusion caused by the incarnation experience. On the lower levels of this plane it is entirely possible to move around remotely in the actual world of form. This area of work falls into the field of 'remote viewing' and has many practical uses.

Remote viewing has often been applied in order to find missing people. Even the police have employed people with an especially strong skill in remote viewing when they have come up against brick walls (and sadly their scepticism often leaves such a move until it is too late to save a life). Even the military have employed remote viewers, though the ethics of using such techniques for military purposes is highly dubious.

Almost everybody is able to astral travel to some degree or another, just as every person is able to walk and run (unless they suffer from a physical disability). However, some people are more naturally gifted in this area than others, just as some people are naturally more gifted runners. Such gifts are not necessarily a sign of spiritual development, in fact those who have developed more beyond this plane will tend to work with it less as they recognise the fragility of the illusion. The emotional plane belongs to the process of incarnation, its elements are left behind to fade on passing back to the spiritual dimensions after death.

The astral plane is a fascinating place. You may even come across others on your travels, some pleasant, some not so pleasant, just as on the physical plane. Bear in mind, though, that this is not the whole reality, not an alternative reality, but only an illusion just as with the physical. Once you develop further and begin to focus more on the mental planes you will find that you can enter the astral whenever you feel the need, but that it will begin to lessen in its fascinations.

LOWER MENTAL PLANE

The Lower Mental Plane is the closest and most open to the astral (emotional) levels and therefore has a profound effect on the emotional functions and, through that level, the physical. It also can block, or misinterpret, energy coming through from the higher mental plane and the spiritual levels beyond that. It is a level that is readily accessible to and open to influence from the conscious mind and is often the most active during hours of sleep and meditation.

Negative thinking can be transmuted into positive with little effort once a decision has been made to make that effort. It takes no more effort to think positive thoughts than negative. However, it is the nature of the human psyche to dwell on the negative as subconsciously it knows that this must be dealt with and balance achieved. This is a problem that can be compounded by the compassionate reaction of sympathy that someone dwelling in negativity receives from others. An undeveloped psyche tends to feed on energy from others, especially when it is given freely, because it is far easier to take another's energy than to find the source within oneself. This is not a conscious decision, or at least not one that most would accept or admit to, but one that brings in the energy it craves through demonstrating a 'poor me' attitude. The more such an attitude is rewarded by energy from others, the easier it is to slip into the habit of seeking attention in the same way on a regular basis. Giving sympathy and energy is not something that is unkind in itself. It is the sign of a compassionate soul to feel for and wish to help those who appear to be suffering from a mental dysfunction. It is not, however, always the best way to help someone overcome such a negative attitude. Helping someone to find a way of asserting themselves in a positive way, seeking the positive aspects of any given situation (and there nearly always is something positive that can be found even in the most dire situations) can, in the long term, be for the best. It can help that individual realise that they don't need to rely on others, acting on them as a vampire, but can tap into the vital energies that we all have access to and continue their growth.

According to Keith Sherwood, 'Research indicates those people with negative attitudes, mental habits and ideas are far more susceptible to cancer (and other disease) . . . The most negative aspects of the cancer personality seem to be a tendency towards self-pity, which goes hand in hand with a very poor self-image. The cancer patient often has an undeveloped capacity to trust either himself or others, which can be traced to early childhood rejection. The cancer patient has a strong tendency to hold anger in and harbour resentment.' By adopting a positive attitude and encouraging the same in those around you, especially if you are involved in healing, is highly beneficial to health on all levels.

As the lower mental plane is most closely associated with the conscious and sub-conscious interface, it follows that conscious effort to tackle the underlying causes of a negative attitude can be very effective, if only the negative attitude itself is willing to accept that it wants to do something about it. There may well be very strong underlying reasons why they are using this strategy to tackle life, and one that is likely to be connected with long-term spiritual development and the activity of karma. The problem may well be rooted deep within the spiritual planes. Wherever that root cause, utilising positive affirmations, or actively deciding to utilise self-hypnosis techniques, are the conscious starting points to progress and growth.

THE SUN

The lower mental plane on the Tree of Life is associated with Beauty (Tipharet) which in turn is associated with the Sun. In the section on the lower emotional plane we saw that the Moon was associated with that plane. The fact that the Sun is associated with a higher plane, in this respect, does not suggest that the God aspects that we use within Wicca and witchcraft are superior – the Goddess works through all the planes and remains the source of all, She just has different ways of manifesting Herself.

Beauty is first witness on the conscious level through the lower mental plane. It is the first time that the light, symbolised by the Sun, illuminates the beauty we can find in life to the conscious mind for our lower selves to appreciate. The energy that is used to develop on the lower mental comes symbolically from the Sun (through it, not entirely of it) and we gradually allow the Light to grow in our hearts and bring warmth and conscious life to our inner selves.

Working Circles through the Sabbats of the year – the Solar cycle – helps to strengthen our connection with the lower mental plane and brings the light of illumination to the things we have learned throughout the year. It enables us to put words to the feelings that have gradually been welling up inside us and to incorporate this growth on all the levels in a conscious way.

The lower mental plane is associated with the heart energy centre. As such it sits in the centre of the body, as it does in the centre of the planes being the fourth, and pumps the energy throughout our systems from the physical, through the emotional, mental and spiritual. The lower mental plane is the level that is the pivotal point between the lower self and what lay beyond in the higher planes. Clarity at this level therefore helps to bring through conscious understanding to our work as witches and Wiccans. It is the central point through which what exists above can communicate with that which exists below and vice versa.

AFFIRMATIONS

Affirmations are similar to prayers. They are positive affirmations that help us to move forward in the world with a more constructive attitude. It is useful to use an affirmation before or after your daily meditations. The key thing with affirmations is to always be positive – that is – use the affirmative! It can also be helpful to write them out first in your journal. Rather than saying things such as 'I need' say 'I have'; rather than 'I want to be' use 'I am'. Never use negative terms. Rather than saying 'I will not be sad' say 'I am perfectly happy', both 'not' and 'sad' are negative words and it is these words that the subconscious will register having taken the words out of the context.

A typical affirmation would normally aim to acknowledge the higher truths that actually every one of us has everything we need within if only we care to look and have the confidence to know. An example of the sort of affirmation I use would be:

> '*Lady and Lord, Goddess and God,*
> *I am of you as you are of me.*
> *This bright a glorious day,*
> *Will be full of joy and happiness,*
> *I will use it to be constructive and bold,*
> *In your honour and in your names.*
> *Blessed Be.'*

THE LIMINAL THRESHOLD

The liminal threshold is the barrier between the conscious and the unconscious function of our brains. It falls between our emotional functions, in which the average person is immersed throughout the bulk of a physical incarnation, and the higher functions of the mental and spiritual bodies. This threshold can prove to be an extraordinarily tough one to break through. The emotional selves create a whole range of delusions that do their best to steer you off course, even when a spiritual understanding and intent has been achieved.

There are, even among the Wiccan community, a great many who have fallen into traps laid down by the emotional selves. For example, many of those who wander around in gothic clothing, carrying fancy wands and sporting enormous pentacles around their necks in public, seem to think that they have reached up towards enlightenment; however in many cases they have actually been diverted by, and expressing elements of their shadow side and a glamour that belongs on the emotional side of the threshold. (This does not intend to imply that such people have not caught glimpses of what lay beyond.) Bear in mind that those immersed entirely in physical materialistic form are looking up and only seeing themselves as the artificial personality side of the lower self. Those who have grown beyond this, having discovered their higher emotional selves, are looking down and tending to see the shadow side of the lower self, but it is still the lower self and not the higher. This is a clue to the nature of the delusion; for growth to continue they need to turn around (metaphorically) and look away from their shadow in order to see the beauty of the greater self.

On the Tree of Life the liminal threshold resides at Tipharet (representing the lower mental plane) just above Hod/Netzach (representing the upper emotional plane).

On death, once the physical body has started to decay, the emotional bodies also begin to drop away. Everything below the liminal threshold is therefore temporary and only part of our incarnation experience. We do not take our emotional functions with us, they are spurious to requirements, though we are, as souls outside of an incarnation, able to recall the emotional memories from any of our life experiences.

MENTAL UNDERSTANDING

One cannot learn how to become a witch of any kind simply from books; neither is it possible to become a Wiccan of any great development simply through practice. There is a great need for balance between both study and practice at all stages from the beginner before even stepping on the path, right through to the most advanced levels. The beginner, if she or he is to make any reasonable progress, needs to understand that Wicca is primarily a spiritual path, a calling to serve the Goddess and God. The more advanced need to build an understanding of the connection between all paths, no matter how diverse they appear, as well as a full appreciation of the more subtle concepts of occult philosophy.

Those at all levels would do very well to dispense with, or at least treat with a large dose of scepticism, most of the growing number of books on spells, charms and general fluff that is passing itself off as witchcraft and Wicca. It is a sign of the growing popularity of, and need for, such a path that the commercial organisations are exploiting the book market; their efforts, however, mainly serve to trivialise and misguide those who have been brought up in a highly materialistic culture. At best, books of 'spells' provide some positive psychological support for those interested in a nature-based spirituality; at worst they are full of pointless love and money spells, methods for 'protection' and invocations doomed to fail. All such ambitions, no matter how well-meaning, belong to that of selfish desire which has no useful place at and beyond the lower mental plane development stage.

The sort of reading material that is highly useful to Wiccans is, sadly, in short supply at the time of writing. There are a lot of books available that have studied the origins of witchcraft, druidry and other native traditions and some of these will help provide a foundation, but we are not living in the past but in the present and looking to the future. It should be appreciated that modern Wicca grew from a broad range of spiritual interpretations for which traditional witchcraft (or the small part that survived) only provided a foundation and cultural framework on which to build. Wicca's founders took a great deal from the work being done by western spiritual esotericists of all kinds, recognising the essential truth in each path whether it is biased towards Christianity, Islam, Buddhism, Hinduism, etc, and filled in the many gaps within the cultural framework that traditional witchcraft provides. By reading the deeper material provided by the Theosophists, Buddhists, occultists and new age thinkers that were growing from the end of the 19th Century, perhaps alongside the works of neopagan authors (and thus learning how to read between the lines of the cultural contexts in which they are written), a mental understanding can be reached that opens many doors in the mind when applying that knowledge in practical terms.

HIGHER MENTAL PLANE

This is the plane on which access to our Higher Self can first be fully accessed. It is where we can uncover access to the full wealth of experience that the Higher Self has stored on this vibrational plane as well as where the plan for our current existence, and all the things we intended to experience during incarnation, is formulated.

It is also to this plane that we are able to partly retreat when we want to stand back and objectively consider how our current life is shaping up, to consider the experiences we have been through and the lessons we may or may not have learnt from those experiences. It is this level that we need enter when we undertake visualisation work. The nature of that work may come to us from our spiritual guides and it is on this level that they tend to contact us, though they themselves are generally focused on the spiritual plane levels. They come down through the planes to meet us half way.

EXERCISE – THE OBSERVER

This is a highly valuable exercise that is worth undertaking from time to time. If you repeat it once a year, keeping the notes safely in your journal, you can look back and compare the notes and see how much our world view has changed. Whilst undergoing a course of spiritual development it often feels that little has changed. Because change

---

happens gradually from day to day, we often forget how we thought or felt just thirteen moons beforehand, and looking back at notes from an exercise such as this will remind us that we have actually progressed far more than we had realised.

You will need four plain sheets of paper, your journal, a pencil or pen, space all around you, and some peace and quiet time for yourself. To do this thoroughly should take no less than an hour, it is best not rushed.

Sit in the middle of a floor and place one piece of paper in each of the directions – north, east, south and west. On the piece of paper in the north write 'physical' in big letters across the top. On the piece of paper to the west write 'emotional'; on the paper to the east write 'mental'; and on the paper to the south write 'spiritual'.

Now turn to face the north in a seated position. Take five minutes or so in meditation to consider your physical needs and desires. You need to be entirely honest with yourself – nobody is going to see what you have written other than yourself. You are only considering physical needs – not any of the others. When you are ready, write down on the piece of paper what you consider to be your physical needs and try to separate out what are real 'needs' from strong desires. You might, for instance, desire larger breasts, or a thinner waist line, but these might not fall into the realm of 'needs'. However, if you are so overweight that you are causing yourself physical problems then losing weight may well fall into the category of 'need'.

When you have done this, next turn to the west and do the same for your emotional needs and desires. When you have meditated and written your notes here, turn to the east and do 'mental' before completing this section of the exercise with 'spiritual'.

The final stage of this exercise is to return to the physical page and face it once more. Have a look at what you have written and meditate a little more. If when you have finished meditating you want to change anything, or add anything, then do so. Then, be totally realistic, consider what you might be able to do to bring about these needs and desires. If you can think of anything, then write it down. If there are items that you realistically cannot bring about then write down why.

Repeat the exercise with the other three pages in the same order as before, then copy your final notes into your journal under the current date.

LOWER SPIRITUAL PLANE

This is the plane on which spirits of all kinds reside. It is the plane on which we can find the 'Summerland' or 'Otherworld' where the spirits of souls who have recently left the physical plane can be found. It is also where our spiritual guides come from, though they tend to lower their vibrations and drop down into the mental planes if they want to communicate something to us. The masters of the elements, the 'Elementals', 'Watchers' or 'Guardians' also belong on this plane, though they too drop down to work on lower planes.

This is the plane on which our own souls, our Higher Selves vibrate. When we are in a state of incarnation they tend to fall into a form of meditative state and return to greater activity when we return from the physical. With practice, through the discipline of regular work on our mediations, it is possible to enter this plane and bring back through the vibrational levels memories stored by our souls – the accumulated wisdom gathered throughout all our lives. It is at this level that our full range of experiences are assimilated and those things of value are kept and added to, through the totality of our experiences (karma), to our level of growth on this plane. It should be remembered that it can take several years of disciplined work to access this level. If you are not ready to enter it then you will not, it will come when you are ready and no amount of conscious forceful effort can over-ride the system. There is a good reason why the memories of past lives and your contacts on the spiritual level do not automatically enter the consciousness on the physical and emotional planes, and this is because if they did, you would be unable to learn new lessons through karma as you would be constantly in mind of previous experiences.

When you are ready, through deep meditation, you may even find that you can enter the memories of those parts of experience between lives, whilst your consciousness is in residence on the lower spiritual plane. In visual terms, this plane can appear in many ways, depending on what your higher mental function chooses. You can create your own reality on this level and delve into any number of the accumulated experiences as source material. This is the beauty of being a free soul – you can be whatever you want to be as long as you have the experience, you can choose to share them and 're-live' them with other members of your soul group.

What does the lower spiritual plane look like? I guess this will be something that different people will experience in different ways. When I have been there I have experienced it as something that is not entirely easy to adequately put into words. As you move beyond the higher mental function one's consciousness appears to witness a realm of pure light. You are aware of other souls all around you, glowing in many 'colours' ranging from yellow to a luminous light blue with the occasional darker hues of blue and purple. You are intimately connected to souls all around you in every way, some of which seem highly active, and others far more docile and working on different planes. In some ways the bubble-style roof of the Eden project in Cornwall, with its transparent hexagonal interfaces is very reminiscent of what I have personally seen. For those who are familiar with this wonderful structure in England, it is far from an adequate analogy, but the closest I can describe. When I have been in this state I have witnessed numerous globular balls of these groups of energies, some closer, some farther away, all interacting in some way or another. It is a very calm and enlightened place, yet very vibrant and active at the same time. I'm sure others will have experienced it in completely different ways and would describe it in completely different terms, but I thought it worth sharing nevertheless. When you first experience this level you may well find that you catch a brief glimpse, then your mental function kicks in to try and rationalise what is happening. By kicking in the conscious, connection with the plane instantly breaks, but with practice, as the mental function learns to relax and go with the flow, the conscious connection gradually becomes easier to maintain.

PAST LIFE REGRESSION

Past life regression is easier than many imagine. It helps, of course, to have developed a reasonable appreciation of the process of life, death and rebirth, but not entirely necessary to fully believe in it as a regression will help to offer answers, or at least raise many questions of such a disbelief. There are very good reasons for the memories of past lives to be left outside of the current incarnation. If we entered life armed with all these memories they would stand in the way of experiencing anything new. The question therefore raises itself as to whether it is right to delve into past life memories or to leave them where they are. To this I would point out that only those memories that we are ready for, as an incarnation, will come to the surface. Those things that are not meant to be, or are unhelpful at this time, remain shrouded and there is no need for undue concern.

While working on the lower spiritual plane we are working just above the higher mental plane. It is between these two planes where the hidden higher knowledge resides. In Kabbalistic terms this is the hidden sephira of Daat. It is this hidden knowledge that occultists aim to uncover and with the force of the higher will apply it with wisdom in service to the gods.

With a past life regression it is best to undertake the work, at least at first, with someone who you fully trust and has a reasonable level of experience. Test the waters first before you cross them and gently work deeper and deeper into the memories as comfort allows. Do not attempt to dive straight into the deep end or get out of your depth, you will sink rather than swim! The following meditation employs a method used in hypnosis where numbers are used to count back, taking you into deeper levels of consciousness. There are many levels and you can continue to work your way down, but remember that you can go so far that it is difficult to find your way back easily. Work one level at a time until you become familiar with it. I tend to work with numbers running down from seven to one. This works for me as I see it as stepping down through the seven sub-planes of each plane and this is how I model my universe. Others may work with different systems and none are necessarily any better than the others – it's what works for you that is important.

In your journey back through life memories you would tend to start with the early ones from your current life. This can take you back to your early childhood and bring up things you thought you had forgotten or not remembered. It is at this stage of your life that you tend to get impressions of the world that stick with you on a sub-conscious level throughout that life. Such memories can, therefore, help to explain why you see things in a certain way and perhaps why you react to certain things the way you do. By bringing these memories to the conscious it means you are then able to analyse such reactions and understand where they came from and, if you don't appreciate such reactions, do something to change things. The simple fact that they have been brought from the sub-conscious into the conscious means that you have created a conscious understanding that often unravels complexes leaving you free of their side effects. Much the same can be said of past life memories. There are experiences buried in our past lives that affect future incarnations and through bringing these things to the surface we can learn and grow significantly.

First of all, ensure you are perfectly comfortable ... When you are ready you are going to close your eyes and take three deep breaths ... Breathing in, fill your lungs with air, continue breathing in until you can breathe in no more ... hold the breath for a moment, then breathe out slowly and completely

... Breathe in again, breathing in deep ... hold for a moment ... then breathe out again ... hold for a moment, then breathe in again deeply, breathing in a pure bright light that fills your entirely body ... as you breathe out, let any dark residues empty out with the breath ... now, just let your breathing settle down to a gentle relaxed rhythm ... breathing in ... and out ... in ... and out.

Before you stands a great oak tree ... look up and see the branches reaching high up into the sky ... become aware of its great roots reaching deep down into Mother Earth ... walk around the trunk of this great tree ... when you come back to where you have started you notice that there is a door in the trunk ... try to pull the door open ... if it opens step inside ... if it refuses to budge just gently bring yourself back to the room and end this visualisation.

As you step inside you notice a number of steps leading down a spiral stairway ... go down these steps counting them as you go ... seven ... six ... five ... four ... three ... two ... one ... the light is not so bright down here, but you notice another set of steps also spiralling down ... you can go down these steps too if you wish, or stay on this level ... the choice is yours as always ... seven ... six ... five ... four ... three ... two ... one.

The light is even less intense on this level, but take note that there are more steps down to take when you feel ready ... for now ... you just sit down on a seat in the wall and close your eyes ... allow your mind to drift back through the years to a time when you are very small ... notice how you feel ... notice what smells there are around you ... notice any sounds ... notice any people that are around you ... make a note of what they are saying ...

When you are ready, in your own time ... let your mind drift back even further ... back to a time before you were born into this life ... back to another existence ... maybe several decades before you were born this time ... maybe even further ... notice how you feel ... notice what smells there are around you ... notice any sounds ... notice any people that are around you ... make a note of what they are saying ... look down at your feet ... what are you wearing? ... look at your legs and hands ... what do you see? ... what are you thinking? ...

When you have had plenty of time to explore this apparently new world ... bring yourself back to the seat deep inside the tree ... you are perfectly calm and relaxed ... stand and begin to walk back up the stairs ... one ... two ... three ... four ... five ... six ... seven ... light begins to get brighter ... now up the next flight of stairs, in your own time ... one ... two ... three ... four ... five ... six ... seven ... finally you move back out through the main door and back outside of the tree ... walk back around the tree the way you came ... begin to notice your breathing again ... allow it to become deeper ... and in your own time, bring yourself back to the room and open your eyes.

Ensure that you are thoroughly grounded. Drink a glass of water if you feel the need. Take some time to write down notes of your experiences in your journal.

HIGHER SPIRITUAL PLANE

The Tree of Life can represent the Higher Spiritual Plane through a single sephira called Keter, meaning Crown. This represents the Divine Source in its first conceivable aspect. The first sign of emanation, where the divine spark of creation enters the realms of possible consciousness. The one without form from which emanate the Goddess and God. There are energies beyond this level, but they are, at the current time, beyond any reasonable comprehension and therefore impossible to describe in any way that would be considered meaningful.

It is from this plane that the higher spiritual guides, those who may be called 'masters' work and direct energies through those in their charge. It is from this level that the driving force of evolution – towards higher states of development – emanates and the energies that inevitably drive all levels of creation towards that development work their way down through the planes creating the inescapable urge in all things to grow. This energy reaches us through our crown function on the physical level, though it affects us in much the same way on the spiritual, mental and emotional levels as well. It is Nature in Her most pure and non-material state. Energies that are pure and powerful have yet to flow through all the planes with clarity, though that is what they are driving towards and will ultimately achieve. It is what lies behind our Higher Will and inevitably directs this will against our lower restrictions caused in the effort to manifest in more pure and unfettered forms in the material plane.

The following examples relate to elements that can be incorporated in ritual to invoke the energies of the Goddess and God. Strictly speaking these belong to the lower spiritual plane. I have included them in this section on the higher spiritual plane as this is the level from which their energies are manifested rather than the level on which they manifest.

CHARGE OF THE GREAT GODDESS

The Charge of the Great Goddess is usually read by the High Priestess during a ritual (the High Priest would normally read the first two lines). This is usually done after the Goddess has been drawn down into

84

the High Priestess and she is speaking as the Goddess. Note that the words contain the secrets of uncovering the mysteries . . . know that if what you are seeking is not found within, then you will never find it without!

Listen to the words of the Great Goddess,
Who throughout time has been known by many names.

Assemble in a sacred place of your own making when the Moon is full,
and any other time you have need of My aid.
Know that My love will make you free,
for nobody can prevent your worship of Me in your mind and your heart.
Listen well when you worship,
and I will teach you the deep mysteries, ancient and powerful.
I require no sacrifices or pain, for I am the Mother of all things,
the Creatress who made you out of My love,
and the One who endures through all time.

I am the beauty of the Earth, the green of growing things.
I am the white Moon whose light is full among the stars and soft upon the Earth.
From Me all things are born, to Me all things, in their seasons return.
Let my worship be in your hearts, for all acts of love and pleasure are My rituals.
You see Me in the love of man and woman, the love of parent and child.
I stand beside you always, whispering soft words of wisdom and guidance.
You need only listen.

All seekers of the Mysteries must come to Me,
for I am the True Source, the Keeper of the Cauldron.
All who seek to know Me, know this.
All your seeking and yearning will be in vain unless you understand the Mystery
that if what you seek is not found within, you will never find it without.
For behold, I have been with you from the beginning,
and I will gather you to my breast at the end.

Blessed Be.

OLD RITUAL OF DARKNESS – INVOCATION OF THE HORNED GOD

The Horned God comes in many guises and under many names – to me He Cernnunos, a dark God of the forest, a protector, the Green Man, consort of the Goddess Cerridwen. To others he may be seen as Pan, a goat-footed God who dances through the forest with his smaller goat horns. He will come to you in whatever guise you expect to see him . . . or maybe he will surprise you! The verse that follows is an invocation

85

for Him, whatever name you may use. It is best incorporated into a ritual within a fully cast and consecrated Circle with the Quarters called at one of the Solar festivals, or Sabbats. It is most effective used late at night, outside in a wood or forest. I include it here as it is a fine example of a traditional Wiccan invocation and another example of the sort of work being undertaken as development on the spiritual planes.

The invocation would normally be read by the High Priest.

By the flame that burneth bright
O! Horned One!
We call thy name into the night
O! Ancient One!
Thee we invite. By the Moon-led-Sea.
By the standing stone and the twisted tree.
Thee we invite, where gather thine own
By the nameless shore, forgotten and lone,
Come where the round of the dance is trod.
Horn and hoof of the goat foot God!
By moonlight meadows on dusky hill.
When the haunted wood is hushed and still
Come to the charm of the chanted prayer.
As the moon bewitches the midnight air
Evoke thy powers that potent bide
In shining stream and the secret tide
In fiery flame by starlight pale.
In shadow lost that rides the gale
And by the ferndrakes, fairy homestead
Of frosts wild and woods enchanted
Come? Come?
To the heart beat's drum!
Come to us who gather below,
When the broad white moon is climbing slow
Through the stars to the heaven's height
We hear thy hoofs on the wind of night!
As black tree branches shake and sigh
Be joy and sorrow we know
We speak the spell thy power unlocks
At Solstice, Sabbat and Equinox

6

THE TREE OF LIFE AND THE TAROT

The Kabbalah is a method of spiritual development that appears to have its origins in the depths of Judaic history, though like so many systems its origins are not entirely clear. Whatever its origins, modern Wicca certainly owes a lot to the Kabbalah and the Tarot which is quite clearly a system within which a great deal of Kabbalistic wisdom is hidden. Wicca's founder, Gerald Gardner, developed his system alongside such luminaries as Aleister Crowley who himself synthesised much from many traditions. Crowley's study of the Kabbalah, as evidenced by his published material on the subject, was considerable. It is a system that is, for those who are drawn to it and for those whose culture it suits, one that is clearly complete and can lead to enlightenment just as many other systems can. In this chapter we shall explore the Kabbalistic links with Wicca, the Tarot's obvious connection with the Kabbalah, and look at how Wiccans can use both the Tarot and some of the Kabbalistic tools as models for understanding and as an aid in development. We shall also look at how the Kabbalah relates to other systems and models of the greater reality and how useful its tools are in explaining certainly elements of that reality.

I would point out here that the Kabbalah is a vast subject and one that can become a lifetime study of great value. All I am able to do in this volume is to offer a brief outline to show its value and show Wicca's connection to it. There are a great many books available on the subject, some from a pagan perspective, if you are interested in further study. The outline in this volume concentrates mainly on the ten sephira. This is a useful starting point, but remember that it is not until the paths between those sephira are understood and worked with that the Tree of Life really comes alive and the depth of the teaching contained within it can be fully appreciated.

THE TREE OF LIFE

The first Kabbalistic glyph to explore is the basic Tree of Life (see Figure 26). It consists of ten sephira that are represented by ten circles or spheres arranged vertically in three columns and horizontally in seven levels (Figure 27). The left hand column relates to the feminine, passive, Goddess principles and can be depicted as a black column. The right

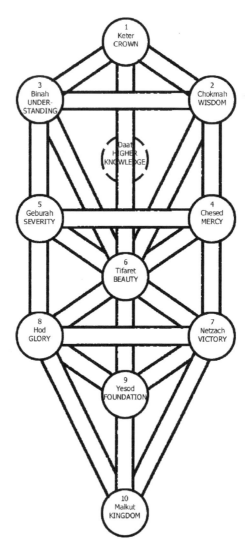

▲ *Figure 26 Hebrew names of the sephiroth with English correspondences and numerical values*

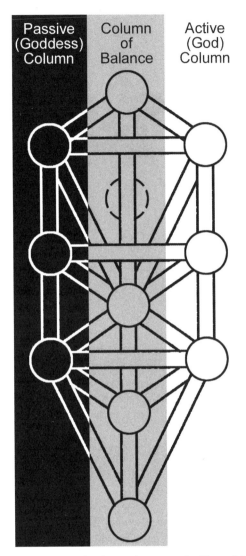

Passive (Goddess) Column **Column of Balance** **Active (God) Column**

▲ *Figure 27 – The three columns on the Tree of Life*

hand column relates to the male, active, God principles and can be depicted as a white column. The central column is the essential balance that those who are to successfully walk any path of spiritual development to its ultimate goal will learn to achieve. On a Wiccan altar these same columns are represented by the Goddess candle on the left (sometimes a black or silver colour), the God candle on the right (sometimes white or gold), and the central candle that represents the divine source from which both emanate.

▲ *Figure 28 – The Pentacle – passive elements on the left and active on the right*

Looking at the Tree of Life's seven levels on a horizontal perspective, we see that they work well as a model of the seven planes of existence (or four with the top three sub-divided into two each). The correspondences on the Tree equate with the physical at the bottom and the spiritual at the top. (There are actually three further levels depicted above the uppermost sephiroth on the Tree of Life that equate with refined concepts of the divine source.)

There is an eleventh sephiroth that is depicted as being hidden (in fact technically it shouldn't even be called a sephiroth at all) that is positioned near the top of the Tree of Life glyph in the centre underneath the uppermost three sephira.

Each sephiroth carries a name and a number. They also carry a whole host of correspondences. The sephiroth are also depicted joined by a number of lines, or paths, twenty-two in all. Each of these paths also carries a name, a number, and correspondences. The paths correspond to the twenty-two cards of the Tarot's major arcana.

Looking at Figure 27 once more we can see that the passive elements on the Tree are on the left and the active elements on the right. This is mirrored in the correspondences attached to the pentacle which has the passive elements of earth and air on the left and the active elements of water and fire on the right (and with the element of spirit in the centre on the line of balance) (Figure 28).

The sets of correspondences for the elements on the Tree of Life can be used to depict an extraordinary array of concepts (see Figure 29), some of which shall be explored later. By working through these correspondences, their relationship to each other, their position in relation to each other, the paths that run between them along with the

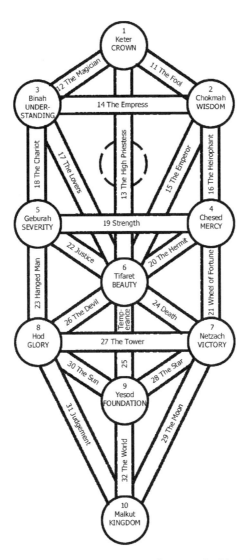

▲ *Figure 29 – The Tarot major arcana correspondences to the 22 paths on the Tree of Life with English names for the Sephiroth*

correspondences of those paths, a highly valuable working model of spiritual development can be determined and used for meditational study and practice.

The Sephira and the paths between them can model all or any part of reality from the microcosmic to the macrocosmic. That is one reason why it is such a useful and successful model. Study of the Kabbalah is a life-time's work (some might say several life-times) and a system complete in itself. It can also be useful, however, as a tool to use as part of other development work. An introduction to the basic meanings of each individual sephira can be found incorporated in Chapter 7 on the 'Seven Planes'. It should be pointed out that whilst the basic Tree of Life and the meaning of the sephira can readily be used to represent the energies of the seven planes, a whole tree can also be associated with each of the levels of physical, emotional, mental and spiritual with the upper and lower divisions marked by the liminal threshold of Tifaret.

THE SEPHIRA

MALKUT – KINGDOM

Malkut stands at the base of the Tree of Life. Its numerical value is 10 and represents the Kingdom corresponding with the physical plane. Malkut is the kingdom of Earth that we have incarnated into in order to learn, to grow and to gradually gain experience so that eventually the planes can merge into one. This is what in Christian terminology would be called 'building Heaven on Earth' and what many might consider to be the underlying plan of the gods that we each play a tiny but essential role in. Malkut is the physical reflection of Keter above from where ultimately the energy flows.

Malkut is often depicted quartered representing the four elements of Earth, Air, Fire and Water. Whilst it represents the Kingdom of Earth it actually represents the entire physical plane which includes the physical Moon, Sun, planets, galaxies and everything else. It is sometimes said that the Tree of Life is actually an upside-down tree with its roots in the spiritual plane which would make Malkut the top of the tree. As with each sephiroth, Malkut has both positive and negative attributes – vices and virtues – as well as a major illusion and obligation. Malkut's vice is inertia where we simply stand still, unable to engage and achieve nothing. Its virtue is the reverse of its vice – activity – which relates closely to its obligation which is discipline which is required in order to maintain activity and grow. Its great illusion is materialism, an illusion that at times seems to rule the entire planet especially within the richest and most powerful nations of the planet.

Keter can be represented by a crowned king, Malkut by a crowned queen. In Wicca She is the Earth Goddess from whose body manifests all that is beautiful on the physical plane.

YESOD – FOUNDATION

Yesod is the first sephira up from Malkut. Its numerical value is 9 and represents the Foundation corresponding with the lower emotional plane. When associated with this plane it represents the two halves of the lower ego – the personality that we present to the world and the shadow that we keep hidden from the world (and often ourselves) though Yesod works on the physical, emotional, mental and spiritual planes as do all the sephiroth. It is the foundation on which all that is built on top of it rests. If the foundation is not strong then it will not provide a strong platform and whatever is developed beyond it is likely to collapse and fall.

Yesod is associated with the Moon and, to a Wiccan, the many names associated with Her as a Goddess in Her triple aspects. Yesod's vice is idleness. Having recognised that there is reality beyond the physical plane those on a spiritual path sometimes discover Yesod and move no further, being to lazy to explore the many other levels of the greater reality. Its virtue is independence which is gained through the virtue of Malkut of discipline. It enables one to be self-governing and requires us not to lean on those around us and, in the process, freeing them to seek their own independence in turn rather than an unhealthy co-dependence. Yesod's illusion, or glamour, is security. Having achieved a strong connection with Yesod, the foundation, they fall for its vice and fail to recognise that the security of a strong foundation requires building upon its strength otherwise the foundation is meaningless and empty. This is related to Yesod's obligation which is trust. Trusting in the Goddess, building on that foundation will enable us to grow no matter what risks we may need to take or how daunting the long road ahead appears.

HOD – GLORY

Hod sits on the passive side of the Tree. Its numerical value is 8 and represents Glory and is one of the two sephiroth that correspond with the higher emotional plane along with Netzach. The glory and splendour of Hod manifests in science, teaching and writing. The messenger gods such as the Celtic Ogma and the Egyptian Thoth are associated with this sphere which has its planetary attribute of Mercury. The energy received from above by Hod enables us to illuminate the truth, to see what is right. This, therefore, is its virtue – truth and its vice is dishonesty and lying either to oneself or those around us. In seeking the truth we must be careful not to delude ourselves by thinking that as we have read every book on a subject then we know everything, for words only contain an interpretation by the person who wrote them and this is only their truth, not yours.

Hod's great illusion is order. Having seen the truth we see that everything must surely be in its place and this is merely yet another self-deception. By recognising this illusion we are then able to work with the next sephiroth representing victory and between the two move up towards Tifaret and beauty, beyond the liminal threshold and restrictions of the emotional planes.

NETZACH – VICTORY

Netzach sits on the active side of the Tree. Its numerical value is 7 and represents Victory and is the other sephiroth that corresponds with the higher emotional plane along with Hod. Victory is an achievement and the Wiccan aspirant who reaches this level is almost certainly ready for the first degree initiation. Netzach encompasses perfect love which works with the perfect trust brought up the path from Yesod to give the aspirant the Wiccan passwords. Whilst Netzach sits on the masculine plane, its correspondence with love and emotions determines its planetary association with Venus and thus with the goddesses such as Rhiannon and Aphrodite.

The virtue of Netzach is unselfish unconditional love and its vice is unchastity which relates not so much to its literal meaning of lustful extra-marital sexual activity but to the vice of impure motivation. Selflessness is a virtue vital to a priestess or priest of the Craft, one that is so often missing. The illusion of this sphere is projection. The unconditional love needs to be directed to your self, not just to others. Projecting one's love onto someone else is no substitute for loving your self and neither is the receiving of love from others.

TIFARET – BEAUTY

Tifaret sits in the centre of the Tree and is very much its pivotal balancing point. Its numerical value is 6 and represents beauty and the lower mental plane. It is associated with the Sun shining down its light from above, reflected by Yesod below that is associated with the Moon. Tifaret is the pivotal point on the Tree, its heart, and is connected to the heart energy centre. It represents beauty and harmony and, as it sits in the centre of the Tree from both a vertical and horizontal perspective, it is also associated with balance and equilibrium. Standing in the middle of the Tree, with the light of the Sun it is easy to see the big picture both above and below having broken through the liminal threshold you can see just how big the Tree is and more fully appreciate the vision of harmony that encompasses it.

Pagan attributes would include those gods associated with the Sun – Lugh, Bel, Llew, Osiris, Ra, Mithra, Dionysus and others, depending on your tradition. One might also place the mythological King Arthur here as he optimises everything that Tifaret represents.

The vice of Tifaret is false pride which relates closely with its obligation of integrity and its illusion of identification. You are who you are, not what you do, and false pride can easily come from an over-blown self-importance. There are many responsibilities as a priestess and priest that require a great deal of giving and shining forth but be careful that this does not give you a false pride as so often happens. You need to learn to walk the talk as well as talking the walk!

Tifaret is also a pivotal point in the Wiccan three degree system and is associated to both the second and third initiations. At second degree Tifaret forms a point on the inverted pentagram given as the symbol for that achievement, but when the pentagram is turned to its upright position it pivots around Tifaret with which it remains in contact, though with perhaps a different relationship.

It should be worth pointing out that the majority of people, even some following a course of spiritual development, rarely progress much beyond the point of Tifaret. Brief glimpses from this position may be possible, but for most they spend much of their lives bouncing around the lower four sephiroth as on a pinball machine. There is nothing wrong with this of course. It takes far more than one life to be able to fully open the channels to Keter whilst still incarnate and even the most respected High Priestess and High Priest of the Craft might only be able to consciously achieve this feat at times. Everyone needs to develop at their own pace at their own time.

GEBURAH – SEVERITY

Geburah sits on the passive side of the Tree. Its numerical value is 5 and represents Severity corresponding, along with Chesed, with the higher mental plane.

Notice that the paths linking to Geburah include Justice and The Hanged Man (below) as well as Strength and The Chariot. Geburah can be considered a very difficult sephira associated with Severity, judgement, fear, but also power and might. The lessons here need to be learned carefully and thoroughly. Wiccans learn to accept that life has many hard lessons, however, and that these hardships and trials bring great strength once they have been worked through that enables further growth and should thus be welcomed as opportunities.

Geburah is associated with the planet Mars, and therefore with any number of the many pagan deities associated with the warrior. Its virtues include courage which is also its obligation – courage to rid ourselves of those things in our life that serve no useful purpose or to sacrifice ourselves for the greater good. However, its vice is wanton destruction, so there is a need as ever to find balance which is included in the path of strength leading to this sephira's balancing opposite of Chesed, meaning mercy. Linked to all of this, Geburah's illusion is invincibility and one ignores this at one's peril!

CHESED – MERCY

Chesed sits on the active side of the Tree. Its numerical value is 4 and represents Mercy corresponding, along with Geburah, with the high mental plane. Greatness is not achieved purely by force and power but also by mercy and grace which is the theme of Chesed.

Its planetary correspondence is Jupiter the great expander of mind and spirit. Notice that the sephira below Chesed, Netzach, was related to perfect love; well Chesed is related to a full understanding of that perfect love with all the things that are required to do so such as mercy and forgiveness. Its virtue is obedience. Having written that I hear a sharp intake of breath! It is not the blind obedience that one might expect of a slave, but the self imposed obedience to undertake the will of the Goddess and God not because you accept their teachings blindly (you should always question everything) but because you are so thoroughly in tune with them that you always agree. This is closely linked with Chesed's obligation of humility.

Chesed's vice is corruption. The corruption of power appears to eventually affect so many people in positions of great responsibility leading to hypocrisy and tyranny. These people generally feel justified in what they do, even when they can see the resulting suffering, and this is closely linked to the illusion of this sphere which is self-righteousness.

BINAH – UNDERSTANDING

Binah sits on the passive side of the Tree. Its numerical value is 3 and represents intelligent Understanding corresponding, along with Chokmah, with the lower spiritual plane. It is the sphere of the Great Goddess, who is known by many names, and corresponds with Saturn. Saturn is associated with restrictions and, as the Great Goddess is associated with form, with the binding together of those things needed to create form.

Binah represents intelligent understanding that comes through being receptive and passive. As with the colour black, it absorbs light and therefore energy but does so in order to be creative. Its virtue is silence. Through silence you can be receptive and therefore Binah could be associated with meditation.

Being always receptive can lead to Binah's vice which is gluttony – taking more than you need. This is related to the obligation to be creative for there needs to be an outlet for all those things that you receive.

The Great Goddess has many attributes. From Her all things are born, but to Her all things in their time return. She is the womb and the cauldron of death and renewal. Death is the illusion of Binah – an illusion because the Goddess ensures that death is not an ending but also a new beginning, a transformation.

CHOKMAH – WISDOM

Chokmah sits on the active side of the Tree. Its numerical value is 2 and represents Wisdom corresponding, along with Binah, with the lower spiritual plane. The Great Goddess sits on the left side of the Tree, therefore Her consort The Great God sits to Her right. Pagans might associate gods such as Odin or the Dagda with this sephira. Chokmah sits at the top of the active column and represents not only wisdom but pure spiritual force as opposed to physical force. He is the great fertiliser and stimulator who works with the Great Goddess to enable form. Chokmah is pure formless force that is constantly moving and unstoppable – as such it can be associated with the wheel of the year, or even the wheel of life. Its virtue is devotion which is inescapable from this position being so close to the pure unfettered source and therefore a vice is not easy to define.

Rather than being associated with a planet, Chokmah is associated with the stars, with the whole zodiac that is in constant motion across the skies bringing energies of many kinds to influence our lives.

KETER – CROWN

Keter sits alone at the top of the Tree. Its numerical value is 1 and represents the Crown corresponding with the higher spiritual plane. Keter represents the source of all things, the first stirrings, the sphere through which pure brilliant light flows in abundance.

Beyond Keter there are three levels which are known as Ain, Ain Soph, and Ain Soph Aur. These are basically 'nothing', 'infinite nothingness', and 'absolute infinite nothingness'. Rather than try to define these concepts, which I basically find impossible, I shall leave you to make the attempt in your meditations which may not result in a workable definition but will almost certainly result in a creative spark of some kind. Keter's virtue is spiritual experience, it has, and cannot have, a vice due to its purity.

DAAT – HIGHER KNOWLEDGE

Daat is not really a sephiroth at all. It sits hidden in between the sephira representing the higher mental plane and the lower spiritual plane directly between Tifaret at the heart of the Tree and Keter at the Crown. It has no numeric value, though it has at times been called the 11th sephiroth, and represents the hidden higher knowledge of the Higher Self. It is hidden only whilst incarnate in order to ensure the higher knowledge, containing the wealth of accumulated experience, does not stand in the way of new experiences.

Daat is experience by a Wiccan, or at least the experience becomes possible, once third degree has been attained although there will be many times before this that an aspirant will think it has been experienced due to all the illusions and glamours on the way. Daat, by it nature, is very personal and each person will experience it in a different way according to their karma accumulated through many lives.

THE WICCAN INITIATION SYMBOLS ON THE TREE OF LIFE

The three symbols used in Wicca to represent the three degrees of initiatory development are the downward-pointing triangle; the downward-pointing pentagram; and the upright pentagram with an upward-pointing triangle above. The fact that these symbols can be superimposed on the Tree of Life Glyph is no accident. Once an elementary study of the meaning of the sephiroth is understood, these symbols quite clearly not only fit neatly onto the glyph, but correspond with the areas of development demanded by the sephiroth that are connected by them as appropriate to the level of initiation represented by each symbol. This was something that was clearly recognised by the occultist Aleister Crowley – they appear as such in some of the drawings he

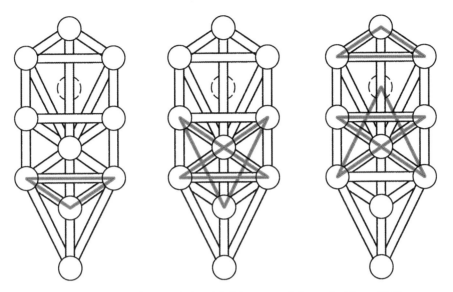

▲ *Figure 30 – The 1st, 2nd and 3rd degree symbols on the Tree of Life*

published of the Tree, and the symbols were introduced (so history would suggest) by Wicca's founder Gerald Gardner who was closely associated with Crowley in the 1940s (see Figure 30).

The downward-pointing triangle, the symbol of a first degree Wiccan, connects with the sephiroth representing the ego of the lower self and two sephira on the emotional level, an area on which first degree Wiccans should endeavour to master.

The downward-pointing pentagram of the second degree Wiccan connects with the ego of the lower self, but also with levels that are higher up than those of the first degree; i.e. with the sephira representing the Goddess and God (using Wiccan terms). At second degree a Wiccan is expected to be fully in touch with the Goddess and God and open to them, though not necessarily to the point where the higher Self has been fully experienced and opened to these energies.

The upright pentagram of the third degree symbol moves the point of the pentagram from the ego of the lower self to that of the higher Self. The triangle above the pentagram that completes the third degree symbol connects the sephira that could be said to represent the Goddess, God and divine source, thus representing the divine union that a third degree should have achieved, symbolised by the Great Rite in that degree's initiation. It should be noted that the position of the downward-pointing pentagram of the second degree, as compared to the position of the upright pentagram of the third, hinges around the sephira of Tifaret (representing beauty, or the realisation of beauty). This fits in well with the Wiccan passwords – perfect love and perfect trust.

THE TAROT

Many people are familiar with the Tarot as a form of divination and this can very extremely useful. However, this is not its only use by any means. It is also useful as a tool for understanding the spiritual growth process and the world around us as its most important (and less well-known) function is as a model of the Tree of Life and the way energy flows around the Tree.

As with the Kabbalah, there can only be speculation as to the origins of the Tarot, but its roots are almost certainly the same as we shall see through our many explorations. I find that the following exercises work best with the standard Rider-Waite deck. There are other decks on the market that show the designers have an understanding of the Tarot as a portrayal of the Tree of Life. Aleister Crowley's Thoth deck is very good for instance (though the 1920s styling can be a little difficult to work with). Crowley was a very worthy magician who heavily influenced several worthy modern esoteric paths, including Wicca – his knowledge of the Kabbalah was highly developed and it is worth obtaining a copy of his book '777' for more advanced study of the Tree of Life and its correspondences. Ellen Reed's *Witch's Tarot* is a good modern 'new age' attempt and is designed specifically with the Kabbalah in mind, in fact she has several excellent books accompanying the pack on the subject especially from a pagan perspective. There are a great many 'new age' style decks on many themes, many highly romantic, that do not appear to display any understanding of the Tree of Life and therefore would seem to miss the Tarot's true meaning. If you feel attracted to any of these decks then by all means try and use them, but be aware that you may discover limitations.

The Tarot consists of 78 cards. This includes the 22 cards of the 'major arcana' and 56 cards of the 'minor arcana'. The major arcana are numbered from 0 to 21. The minor arcana consist of 4 suits – pentacles, cups, swords and wands. These suits relate to the seven planes. The pentacles relate to the physical plane, the cups to the lower and upper emotional planes, the swords to the lower and upper mental planes and the wands to the lower and upper spiritual planes. Each suit in the minor arcana has cards numbered from ace (1) to 10 plus four 'court cards' being the page, knight, queen and king (in the Rider-Waite deck). The cards numbered from 1 to 10 relate to correspondingly numbered sephira on the Tree of Life. The court cards relate to action and movement on the Tree.

You will find it useful to take a good look through the whole pack of cards from time to time and study the images in detail in order to build a complete familiarity with the deck. Take note of the colours as well as the images and begin to consider the symbolic meaning that could be attached to the images.

You will find it useful to either make notes in your journal, or perhaps (if you choose) to start a separate journal dedicated entirely to your study of the Tarot).

EXERCISE – THE TAROT'S MAJOR ARCANA AS AN AID TO INITIATORY DEVELOPMENT

Cut ten circles out of card or paper. Number them from one to ten and write the names of the sephira on them and any number of correspondences you may discover. Lay them out on the floor in the correct order and pattern for the Tree of Life. Using the twenty-two major arcana cards from any Tarot pack, lay the cards on the floor between the sephira in the correct position for the paths on the Tree. By studying the sephira and their correspondences see how the images on the paths give you clues to the development requirements. Where do you feel you are strongest? Where do you feel there is a need for more inner work? Where would you place yourself on the Tree? Are you sure? (The person who hesitates before answering the question 'are you sure?' is most likely to give an honest answer.) Meditate on this! How does this position compare to your degree of initiation?

THE FOUR TREES AND THE TAROT'S MINOR ARCANA

We have already seen how the Tree of Life in its simplest form provides a useful model of the seven planes, the three pillars, and whole range of esoteric concepts to be discovered with further study. Another useful, and more elaborate, development of the Tree of Life theme is the glyph known as 'The Four Trees', sometimes known as the 'Four Worlds', or even 'Jacob's Ladder' (see Figure 31). This comprises four individual

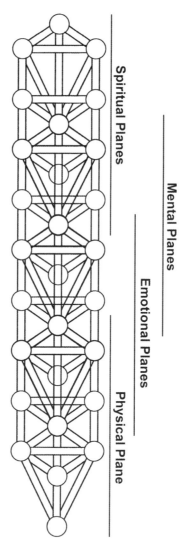

▲ *Figure 31 – The Four Trees representing the planes of the physical, emotional, mental and spiritual overlap each other. Note how the Daat of the lower plane becomes the Yesod of the one above it*

Tree of Life glyphs built one on top of the other and overlapping so that the Malkut of the second tree begins at the Tifaret of the one below in each case. These four trees represent the physical, emotional (astral), mental and spiritual planes. The Four Trees provide us with an even more refined model of the planes and an even greater breakdown of the levels through which we need to work if we are to fully achieve the knowledge and wisdom that leads to spiritual development at its most fulfilling levels.

The minor arcana cards of the Tarot provide us with a model of the Four Trees. In fact the Tarot may well have been devised as a means of preserving the wisdom of the Kabbalah, the Tree of Life and the Four Trees in pictorial form (though this is hotly denied in some quarters). The Tarot can indeed be a valuable tool for divination, but its use in Kabbalah is probably of far greater value. The pentacles of the minor arcana correspond with the sephira of Jacob's Ladder on the tree representing the physical plane. The cups correspond with the tree representing the emotional planes; swords with the mental planes and wands with the spiritual planes. The cards numbered one to ten in the minor arcana match up to the sephiroth in the same order as the number system on the Tree of Life. That is, the ace of each suit matches up to Keter on each tree element on the Ladder and the ten of each suit matching up with the Malkut with all the other cards matching up appropriately in between.

By working with the tarot cards in this layout it is easy to see how readily the cards match the correspondences of the Sephiroth, how the correspondences vary from plane to plane, and the inevitable ebb and flow of the process of moving through those planes during development.

EXERCISE – THE TAROT'S MINOR ARCANA ON THE FOUR TREES

- Remove the 22 major arcana cards from the Tarot pack.
- Remove all the court cards from the pack (i.e. the kings, queens, pages and knights.
- Divide the pack into the four suits (pentacles, swords, wands and cups).
- Put each suit into numerical order with ace on the bottom) so that you have four piles of suit cards with the ten of each suit on the top.
- Pick up the pentacle cards. Lay each of the cards in a Tree of Life pattern so that the number on the card matches the numerical value of each sephira. You should then have ten cards with the ten of pentacles in the position of Malkut, with the ace of pentacles depicting a crown at the top in the Keter or 'Crown' position.
- Take some time to study the images on the cards.

Look to see how the images match up with the many correspondences of the sephiroth. You have in front of you a route map of the process required to be trodden on the physical plane depicted in symbolic form by the images on the cards. The route shows the path to be trodden and the revelations discovered in the appropriate order for one travelling an esoteric path of practically any kind. However, this is only the physical plane. We also have the emotional or astral planes, the mental planes, and the spiritual planes to be considered. We already have the physical plane laid out in front of us in the form of the pentacle cards. The emotional plane will be depicted by the cup cards, the mental by the swords and the spiritual by the wands.

The other planes now need to be fitted into the model we have started. They do not fit directly over the other cards, nor are they arranged above each other, but overlap as they do in reality. If with look at the images on the pentacle (physical plane) cards, we see that by the time we get to the Tifaret (Beauty) position we have learnt that the physical plane, and all the material riches that come with it) need to be shared amongst ourselves in a balanced fashion. It is in the position, and at this stage of development, that the Malkut of the emotional (astral) plane kicks in. The cup cards are therefore laid out in a Tree of Life pattern with the ten of cups being placed on top of the six of pentacles and working upwards to a new crown – the crown of the emotional plane depicted by the ace of cups.

- Take the suit of cups cards.
- Place the ten of cups on top of the six of pentacles.
- The next card, the nine of cups, is placed in the position of Daat (Knowledge) of the pentacle layer (thus revealing the emotional secret of the physical plane) and the rest of the cards complete the pattern.
- Take time again to study the images on the cards and see how they match up with their own corresponding positions on the Tree of Life, but also how they relate to the pentacle (physical plane) cards that they overlap.

You can then proceed to complete this new model by repeating the process with the sword (mental plane) cards and the wand (spiritual plane) cards.

You now have laid the cards out in a glyph know as 'Jacob's Ladder'. It is an even more elaborate and accurate layout of the planes of existence. Within it there are many hints, tips, lessons and revelations that can be used, especially through meditation, to build a fuller understanding of the four planes and the path that needs to be trod towards enlightenment. The four planes in this case represent the seven planes if one divides the emotional, mental and spiritual planes into two halves (divided into upper and lower by the Tifaret position. This model will be found particularly useful if just small sections are taken for meditation at any one time. There is so much information here it would be futile to expect to understand but a small fraction in any one sitting.

If you want to take this exercise a stage further you can retrieve the court cards that you removed from the Tarot pack. These cards represent activity on the Ladder. Try to place these cards in positions that correspond according to your own level of development and understanding and see what clues and options are revealed for further development.

TAROT'S MAJOR ARCANA

EXERCISE[3] – THE MAJOR ARCANA AS ELEMENTAL ARCHETYPES

This exercise is particularly effective when conducted within a physically or astrally cast circle. Take time to prepare the Circle and introduce the witch's tools (athame, wand, chalice and pentacle) as appropriate.

- Remove the twenty-two major arcana cards from the Tarot deck.
- Remove the 'fool' card (numbered zero) and lay it in front of you. This card represents the attitude that you should adopt in your approach to the Tarot, and indeed spiritual growth. Meditate on the image, witness its childlike inner wisdom, the representation of adventure and the carefree way the precipice is approached.
- Now take the 'magician' card (numbered one) and place it about one yard in front of you. Study this card. The image shows a magician with symbols of the four elements that are used in

---

[3] Note – The numerical values assigned to the major arcana in this exercise are as found on the standard Rider-Waite Tarot deck. If you use a different pack you may, or may not, find that the numerical values vary (as does the symbolism found on the cards).

Wicca (and other paths) – the pentacle, the sword, the cup (or chalice) and the wand. The figure points both to the spiritual plane (symbolically above) and the physical plane (symbolically below). The 'magician' is fully in control of the elements as well as fully in touch with the spiritual and physical. The 'magician' represents you standing in the middle of the Circle.

- Now take the 'strength' card (numbered eight), the 'justice' card (numbered eleven), the 'temperance' card (numbered fourteen), and the 'world' card (numbered twenty-one).
- Place the 'world' about a foot in front of the 'magician' (in the north – earth position), the 'justice' card to the right (in the east – air position), the 'strength' card underneath the 'magician' (in the south – fire position), and 'temperance' to the left (in the west – water position).
- The characters and symbols represented on the four cards that now mark the four cardinal points represent the guardian masters of the four elements of earth, air, fire and water, with the 'magician' representing your spirit in the middle of the Circle. In their turn the cards in the four quarters, and those we are going to associate with them, represent the four planes (earth – physical, water – emotional (astral), air – mental, and fire – spiritual).
- Meditate for a while on this Celtic Cross arrangement. Visualise yourself standing in the place of the 'magician', as the magician, with the guardian masters facing you from each quarter. Now turn to face the south and approach the character representing 'strength' card in the south. As you approach you are invited to walk through a gateway.
- Place the cards numbered two, three, four and five ('high priestess', 'empress', 'emperor', and 'hierophant') around the 'strength' card. These are the guardians of fire in their five guises. They represent five ways of expressing power. The 'High Priestess' represents inner wisdom intuitively expressed – the power to look within and beyond the veil, the keeper of the law. The 'Empress' represents outwardly expressed and cultured feminine power – the mother figure with the caring, nurturing and protecting attributes associated with that archetype. The 'Emperor' represents outwardly expressed masculine power – the strength of the father figure, self-confidence (especially around authority figures). The 'Hierophant' (High Priest or 'Pope') represents inner wisdom expressed outwardly as pure spiritual power, a sage, counsellor, or guide.

- Meditate with each of these cards in turn and then consider the cards together and experience how they each represent power expressed and used in different ways as appropriate to any given situation. They represent the fire within and without.
- Now take your leave of these characters and move back through the gateway to stand once again in the middle of the Circle. Contemplate what you have just discovered and make some notes if required.
- Now turn to face west and approach the character representing the 'Temperance' card. She stands pouring water from one cup to the other with one foot in the water and the other on earth. This represents the overlap between the physical and emotional planes. As you approach you are invited to enter through another gateway.
- Place the cards numbered six, seven, nine and ten (the 'Lovers', the 'Chariot', the 'Hermit', and the 'Wheel of Fortune') around the 'Temperance' card. These are the guardians of water in their five guises. They represent five ways of expressing emotional energy. The 'Lovers' (depicted with the Venus – the Goddess of Love) represents the healing power of love with the balance of masculine and feminine. The 'Chariot' represents a more singular expression of success and progress, forging forward boldly at times of possible difficulty. The 'Hermit' (depicted carrying the staff of wisdom and an upraised lantern to light the way forward) represents the inner emotional peace, teaching patience within for all travellers on a spiritual path. The 'Wheel of Fortune' represents the cycles of life with all its ups and downs. It represents the emotional wisdom of going with the flow of those changes, rather than resisting them, being gracious in times of victory and humble in times of defeat.
- Meditate with each of these cards in turn and then consider the cards together and experience how they each represent emotion expressed and used in different ways as appropriate to any given situation. They represent the water within and without.
- Now take your leave of these characters and move back through the gateway to stand once again in the middle of the Circle. Contemplate what you have just discovered and make some notes if required.
- Now turn to face east and approach the character representing the 'Justice' card. She sits on a throne with the sword of justice in one hand and a balance in the other. As you approach you are invited to enter through another gateway.

- Place the cards numbered twelve, thirteen, fifteen, and sixteen (the 'Hanged Man', the 'Devil', 'Death', and the 'Tower') around the 'Justice' card. These are the guardians of air in their five guises. They represent five ways of expressing mental energy. They show five, quite awesome, figures that should not be approached in an attitude of fear. The 'Hanged Man', despite his apparent predicament, is perfectly at ease – this represents self assurance and an inner conviction that we are doing what is intuitively right with a strength of will to serve appropriate on the mental plane. The 'Devil' represents the many illusions (or glamours) that we will be faced with on the path – the follies, the dweller on the threshold who demands we ruthlessly face and accept our faults (hidden on our shadow side) so that we can break through and move forward. 'Death' represents the natural and rightful end, and the coming to terms with the death of things we treasured in a mental way – this character helps to evaluate what has passed so that we are strengthened to face what is ahead in a new cycle. The 'Tower' represents the lightning strike that shatters our illusions (or glamours) as each new revelation burns away the misconceptions of those that we had held on to. The crown on the top of the tower lifts to welcome this cleansing and renewal, with the contents of that tower burnt away while its form remains standing tall – the lightning strike represents the mental inspiration that can transform if we allow it to.
- Meditate with each of these cards in turn and then consider the cards together and experience how they each represent what can be experienced as mental torments expressed in different ways as appropriate to any given situation. They represent the air within and without.
- Now take your leave of these characters and move back through the gateway to stand once again in the middle of the Circle. Contemplate what you have just discovered and make some notes if required.
- Place the cards numbered seventeen, eighteen, nineteen, and twenty (the 'Star', the 'Sun', the 'Moon', and 'Judgement') around the 'World' card. These are the guardians of earth in their five guises. They represent five influences that we experience on the physical plane. The 'Star' represents the Star Maiden – the Goddess Arianrhod perhaps – pouring the influences of the stars upon the physical plane, the sea and the earth. This gives us a clue

as to the influences coming to us that will help us fulfil our life plan and the lessons we hoped to learn from it with the astrological energies chosen by us for our birth – our true destiny. The 'Sun' represents the light and warmth of the spirit that animates us along with an awareness of our higher selves and our guardians. The 'Sun' represents the way we present ourselves to the world in the light of day and through the way that energy works through us. The 'Moon' represents the opening up of our psychic connections to the physical plane – the realm of dreams and visuals brought down to earth from the emotional plane. 'Judgement' represents the awakening on the physical plane from our spiritual sleep – the transformation that arouses us from physical lethargy to seek new horizons and opportunities.

- Meditate with each of these cards in turn and then consider the cards together and experience how they each represent emotion expressed and used in different ways as appropriate to any given situation. They represent the water within and without.
- Now take your leave of these characters and move back through the gateway to stand once again in the middle of the Circle. Contemplate what you have just discovered and make some notes if required.
- Take time to go back though any of the gateways at any time meditating and taking notes as ideas come to mind.

If you have conducted this exercise in a cast Circle, remember to clear the Circle appropriately at the end. This is an exercise within which is hidden a great deal of knowledge and wisdom. Trying to take too much in during one sitting may well result in confusion as the mind needs time to assimilate. You would therefore, most likely, find it of value to repeat this exercise at intervals and refer back to notes of your previous sections and see how your perceptions and understandings modify themselves and develop.

7

CALENDAR AND THE PAGAN WHEEL OF THE YEAR – A REVISION

For those following a nature-based path, following the changes that come with the seasons is clearly a fundamental element within the spiritual system. In its simplest form this ensures the individual builds a close relationship, often lost due to modern living, with what is often seen as the Earth Goddess, Moon Goddess and Solar God. This relationship is central to Wiccan spirituality.

Most modern pagans, whether Wiccan or otherwise, have adopted an eight-spoke wheel of the year as in Figure 32. The eight-spoke wheel has been repeated in various forms by numerous authors throughout the world over and over again even though there is no historic record of any of our ancestors having used an eight-fold division. (It should be pointed out that this eight-fold division was even adopted by Wiccan founders such as Gardner and Sanders having referenced the system from the same misinterpreted sources.) The eight-fold division does not follow the natural cycles accurately and is based on a serious misinterpretation of historic records that have probably been confused by the changing calendar systems over the last few thousand years. Just because the system has been repeated parrot fashion by numerous authors, including some of the most respected and influential, does not make it correct. It is certainly not helpful to the neopagan aspirant to be following a system that fails to fully connect with the wheel as it turns.

Many of the neopagan paths are based on what is known of the history of the Celts. The only reasonably complete historic record of a Celtic calendar to have survived is the Coligny Calendar. This basically appears to shows a twelve-fold division of the year based on the solar cycle interlaced with the lunar cycle. It is unclear which of the modern authors first mooted an eight-fold division, but the concept is almost

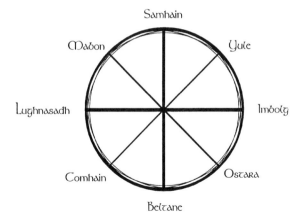

▲ *Figure 32 – The eight festivals generally adopted in recent years as the pagan Wheel of the year. The Major Sabbats are generally celebrated on fixed dates. Samhain (Halloween, 31st October); Imbolg (Candlemass, 1st or 2nd February); Beltane (May Day, 1st May); Lughnassadh (1st August)*

certainly based on the research published by J R Frasier in *The Golden Bough*. Frasier didn't, however, define an eight-fold division. All he did was to record dates of festivals that had survived into the records of his time and were still being practised by various cultural groups. By extrapolating the dates from his work it is certainly possible to find eight common festivals held around certain dates on the calendar. What is not taken account of is the fact that the calendar in use at various times in history has shifted due to the inaccuracies of the calendar system imposed on society by the Roman Catholic Church.

There is evidence, for instance, that 10th century Druids in Cornwall marked Beltane on 1st May. In the 10th century the system being used to calculate days was the Julian calendar. Since then, in order to 'correct' the calendar (or rather to realign it to the concept of the solar year devised by the first Christian pontiff Constantine) 11 days were removed from the calendar by Pope Gregory in the 16th century to form the Gregorian system used today. This involved shifting 21st March (determined by Constantine to be the date of the spring equinox) back in line with the solar cycle. This means that 1st March being celebrated as Beltane in the 10th century is not the same 1st March in our present calendar; in fact it would have been much closer to the date when the Sun moved from Aries into Taurus. It is quite possible also that the cattle they were recorded to have driven between two bonfires symbolically represented Taurus the bull.

Neopagans tend to mark the beginning of the wheel at different points depending on their tradition and their own interpretation. Some might use the mid-winter solstice, others the movement of the Sun into Aries (the beginning of the zodiacal cycle), others still might use Samhain. It is not particularly important where any individual marks the beginning of the year: a wheel in reality has no beginning or end but just keeps turning. However, those using Samhain tend to mark it as a major sabbat beginning at sunset on 31st October. Why? 31st October cannot be related to anything in the natural cycle, and yet it is, to many, a major sabbat and one of the most important in the wheel. Celebrating Samhain as the beginning and end of the year tends to be based on the Celtic tradition, but it is surely important to get the date right!

The Celts almost certainly inherited the system of marking Samhain and Beltane as the two most important dates in the Wheel from the earliest of pagan systems. The earliest calendars, it would appear, were based on stellar observations. The Babylonians used, as their reference points, the axis of the star Aldebran (the bull's eye in Taurus) and the star Antares (in the heart of Scorpio) that were opposite each other in the zodiac circle of the cosmos. Later on, the Egyptians were using a 360-day year (hence the 360 degrees in a circle) to which they had to add days in order to make adjustments. The beginning of the Egyptian wheel of the year began with the rise of Scorpio. By the later Egyptian period, the Greeks, who were also great mathematicians and astrologers, were using a lunar-based calendar system known as the Metonic Calendar (devised by Meton of Athens around 440 BCE). This used the lunar months (or 'moonths') in a 19 solar year 'Metonic Cycle' of 235 lunar months. At the end of this cycle the moons begin to fall on (almost) the same solar dates of the year. (This should not be confused with the moon's periodic cycle of 18 years 11.3 days which has important significance in the maturation of our physical incarnations.) By this time, spirituality was already becoming more male-dominated and thus more Solar oriented. Instead of beginning the year in Scorpio the Greek astrologers developed a system that began the year with the sprouting forth of Aries at the spring equinox. This is why Aries is used as the first symbol in the astrological calendar in the most common form of the modern western astrological wheel. The spring equinox determines the point of Aries in the astrological calendar (from which the other twelve points follow) even though currently the astronomical observations (as opposed to astrological) show that this is no longer the case due to the precession of the equinoxes.

To cut a long story short the Celtic Wheel of the Year should be based on the twelve-fold division used today as the astrological wheel as it is in the Celtic Coligny calendar. Samhain should more properly marked as the Sun moves from Libra to Scorpio (the scorpion most appropriately being a creature associated with death) and Beltane as the Sun moves from Aries to Taurus. The solstices and equinoxes remain the same and the other festivals shifted accordingly reviving four festivals missed out of the eight-spoke wheel.

By reviving the twelve-spoke wheel in line with the astrological system we also find lots of other things fall into place. Each of the four major sabbats, for instance, falls as the Sun moves into a sign associated with fixed elements of Earth, Air, Fire and Water. The equinoxes and solstices fall as the Sun moves into the cardinal signs of each element and the four missing festivals as He moves into the mutable signs of each element.

As a Wiccan, I consider it is important if not vital to maintain a balance between Goddess and God as this is a defining element of the whole system. Whilst I mark the moment of the movement of the Sun from one sign to another, I tend to celebrate as the Moon reaches Her full within each month whilst honouring the God cycles at each of the solstices. As an occultist I also make use of the planets and the seven ray energies that flow through them as they move through the zodiac affecting us in so many subtle but important ways. The diagram below (Figure 33), therefore, forms part of the symbolic pentacle that I work with – the pentagram representing the elements, the seven-pointed star representing the plants and the twelve-fold division representing the Wheel.

Those who wish to continue using the eight-fold wheel have, of course, every right to do so. It is just worth bearing in mind that half of the festivals (the major ones) in that system fall on a date that has no natural relevance and, to make matters worse, there are four festivals not being marked at all!

THE TWELVE-SPOKE WHEEL OF THE YEAR

If we once again refer back to the Celtic Coligny Calendar we can see that the original pagan wheel of the year is based on a twelve-spoke wheel rather than an eight, as has been discussed above. The Coligny Calendar (Table 3) is an elaborate affair that shows our ancient Celtic pagan ancestors had a reasonably advanced knowledge of astronomy and a

▲ *Figure 33 – Pentagram representing the elements surrounded by the influences of the planets and the zodiac*

good understanding of the movement of the Sun and Moon. In fact their system was far more advanced than that used in the dark ages many hundreds of years later! Unfortunately the precise meaning of the names of these twelve festivals has survived only in Gaulish and the

Table 3 – The Celtic Coligny Calendar

Month	Coligny name	Zodiac	Neo-pagan festival
23rd Oct–22nd Nov	Samonios	Scorpio	Samhain
23rd Nov–21st Dec	Duannios	Sagittarius	
22nd Dec–20th Jan	Riuros	Capricorn	Yule
21st Jan–18th Feb	Anagantios	Aquarius	Imbolg
19th Feb–20th March	Ogronios	Pisces	
21st Mar–20th April	Cutios	Aries	Ostara
21st April–21st May	Giamonios	Taurus	Beltane
22nd May–21st June	Simivisonios	Gemini	
22nd June–22nd July	Equos	Cancer	Comhain
23rd July–23rd Aug	Elembiuos	Leo	Lughnasadh
24th Aug–22nd Sept	Edrinios	Virgo	
23rd Sept–22nd Oct	Cantlos	Libra	Mabon/Lamass

precise meanings of these words remains somewhat obscure. Even if a precise translation were available it is almost certain that they would relate to annual practices of the time such as horse trading, the harvest cycle, tax collections etc., and these would not be entirely relevant to the modern era anyway. For the sake of completeness the Gaulish names have been included alongside the approximate dates used in the modern Gregorian Calendar used in the West today and the names of the Greek Zodiac with which most people are familiar. (NB For precise dates and times of the Sun's movements associated with the modern it is necessary to check with an ephemeris.)

To me, especially with the absence of any leading body in Wicca, it is important that each person, or each coven, adopts a specific procedure to marking these festivals. One could mark each one on the actually date the Sun passes into the astrological sign. Perhaps a better way would be to mark the solstices and equinoxes at the time of the Sun's rise on the actual date, but to mark the others on the first full-moon when the Sun has moved into that sign, whilst recognising or marking the actual date of that movement in some way. This will give you a strong connection between the Solar cycle and its interrelationship with the Lunar cycle — all important in a nature-based path, especially in Wicca in which we relate to the interaction between Goddess (symbolised by the Moon) and God (symbolised by the Sun).

How you celebrate this cycle is obviously a matter of personal choice. I prefer and enjoy elaborate and full-blown ritual (though there are times when I mark the event quietly). However, it is important that you do what feels right for you. If you don't enjoy elaborate rituals then don't do them! Lighting an appropriate coloured candle and meditating with it for a short time may be entirely adequate for your own needs whilst reserving a special ritual either for when the mood takes you, or for making the most of the more important festivals in the cycle such as Samhain, Yule, Beltane, and the Summer Solstice.

HERBS, INCENSES, COLOURS AND OTHER SYMBOLS FOR THE WHEEL OF THE YEAR

Adopting certain herbs and incenses and other natural materials for each festival also helps to strengthen the connection with the annual cycle and raise the appropriate energies required for our work. In the 21st century we have the luxury of having access to a ready supply of some of the most wonderful incenses imported from across the world. Frankincense, for instance, is a gum that has been prized for many centuries by occultists (amongst others) for its spiritual qualities even though it is mainly obtained from the Middle-East and north Africa. I highly recommend these incenses, but also suggest that it is important to incorporate herbs that are native to your part of the world and that fit well with the seasonal energy.

Colours are also associated with the Wheel of the Year and the astrological signs. They run through the colour spectrum from red through to purple. Using the Greek system which begins the year in Aries, they represent a growth cycle that corresponds with the colours associated with the major energy centres (chakras) with magenta in Pisces preparing the way to bring the Wheel back full circle in Aries with scarlet red again.

Table 4 offers a traditional association of herbs and incenses, alongside the colours against the twelve-spoked Wheel. You may well find it valuable in focusing your energies to incorporate these incenses and colours into your work. You could, for instance, incorporate the colour associated with your Solar birth sign into your working robes. It is interesting, or perhaps just natural, that more often than not the colours associated with one's Solar birth sign is one that you find quite appealing.

Table 4

Astrological sign	Symbol	Herb/incense	Colour
Scorpio	♏	Opopanax, pine, clove	Blue-green
Sagittarius	♐	Aloes, cedar, anise, juniper	Blue
Capricorn	♑	Benzoin, honeysuckle, patchouli, magnolia	Blue-black
Aquarius	♒	Euphorbium, lavender, mint, acacia	Violet
Pisces	♓	Red storax, jasmine, sage, iris	Magenta
Aries	♈	Myrrh, rosemary, thyme	Scarlet
Taurus	♉	Pepperwort (Dittany), apple, mugwort, daisy, cardamom	Red-orange
Gemini	♊	Mastic, clover, dill, meadowsweet	Orange
Cancer	♋	Camphor, agrimony, lemon balm, lilac	Gold
Leo	♌	Frankincense, saffron, sunflower, eyebright	Yellow
Virgo	♍	Sandalwood, fennel, mace, bergamot	Chartreuse
Libra	♎	Galbanum, rose, orchid, marjoram	Green

8

PLANETARY AND ZODIACAL INFLUENCES

Blessed be Arianrhod, Queen of the Silver Wheel

This chapter studies the esoteric symbols, the pagan significances, and the nature of the energies from the planets within our solar system and the stars. It is not intended as an instruction on drawing an astrological birth chart or to provide a detailed understanding of everyday astrology. As useful as these subjects are, to a witch in particular, everyday astrology can be studied more fully in one of the many excellent books specifically on that subject.

Many people accept that the position of the planets against the background of the constellations has a profound affect on each individual's character from the time of birth. Also that the ever changing energies caused by the interaction of those planets, against the background of the constellations, affects each individual in different ways according to that character in our everyday interactions on the physical plane. Building up a fuller appreciation of how these energies work together it is possible to better understand ourselves and those around us, and to work with those energies to help fulfil the challenges we have set ourselves in this current life. When we are born into a physical incarnation, the energies of the planets at that time are imprinted into our physical and emotion bodies and we carry that pattern, which manifests as character, through to death where it is then left behind. The position of the planets at the birth of our current incarnation, creating that imprint, are chosen to best suit those challenges that we need to overcome in order to grow and develop. Having chosen a certain make up, the planets, as they constantly change their positions in relation to us, to each other and the zodiac, guide us in certain directions. It is because of such guidance that even the least spiritually developed of individuals is able to gradually grow on the physical plane towards a conscious relationship with the Higher Self. The process may take several

117

lifetimes, but the guidance is there and influencing all of us whether we are conscious of it or not.

In order to build up an understanding of the energies that are at play through the planets and there positions, it is helpful to study some of the individual elements and concepts. Once a reasonable understanding has been developed, we can then move on to start working more consciously with those energies and using them to aid us in our work as a Wiccan.

On a clear night we are honoured to be able to view the stars. Each star forms a glittering jewel in the gown of the Goddess Arianrhod. The sky forms the great Silver Wheel on which Arianrhod spins the energies into a complex web of which we are but a tiny part. There is an intelligence behind the work. It is an intelligence that we cannot entirely comprehend, at least from the limitations of being in a physical form, but there is an intelligence nevertheless. It is not an intelligence that we can explain entirely satisfactorily by visualising it in anthropomorphic form, but this is the best that we can do and suffices for most. Whilst we witness the cosmos through our physical eyes, registered by our brains, the energies permeate all of the planes – the physical, emotional, mental and spiritual. The stars and planets are only physical manifestations of a greater reality in exactly the same way that each of us, as incarnations, are only physical manifestations of a greater reality. The energies that we work with do not come directly from the physical planets, but through them from beyond the physical. The planets' position in relation to the zodiac serves to modify those energies just as a coloured lens modifies the light flowing through it. For this reason it may be useful to start with a look at the twelve zodiacal signs.

SIGNS OF THE ZODIAC

In order to put some form onto these energies, the sky (or more accurately the part of the sky that corresponds with the apparent path of the Sun – the 'ecliptic') is physically divided up into twelve constellations – Aries, Taurus, Gemini, Cancer, Leo, Virgo, Libra, Scorpio, Sagittarius, Capricorn, Aquarius, and Pisces (see Table 5). Throughout history there have been many allegorical myths devised in an effort to explain these energies in story form that our lower mental abilities find easier to appreciate. In the Judaic Old Testament they are the twelve brothers of Joseph. In the New Testament they are the twelve disciples of Jesus. In Celtic mythology they are the twelve knights of Arthur's round table. In each case there is a central character being influenced by energies of

Table 5 – Symbols used for the signs of the Zodiac

Aries	♈	Libra	♎
Taurus	♏	Scorpio	♏
Gemini	♊	Sagittarius	♐
Cancer	♋	Capricorn	♑
Leo	♌	Aquarius	♒
Virgo	♍	Pisces	♓

twelve others around him (in relatively modern mythology I regret it is usually a 'him' – a product of the Piscean Age). In an ideal Wiccan Circle the twelve are represented by coven members who generally work around the High Priestess who becomes the focus of each of the coven member's energies.

Each of the constellations used in astrology has its own characteristics. Each is assigned one of the elements of Earth, Air, Fire or Water – three to each. Each is ruled by a planetary energy. Each is assigned a quality of mutable, cardinal or fixed, one of each to the sets of three constellations assigned each of the four elements. Each is also given a masculine or feminine attribute. This is shown in Table 6.

Table 6 – Elements, qualities, gender attributes and planetary rulers associated with the signs of the Zodiac

Planetary body	Element	Quality	Masculine/ Feminine	Planetary ruler(s)
Aries	Fire	Cardinal	Masculine	Mars
Taurus	Earth	Fixed	Feminine	Venus
Gemini	Air	Mutable	Masculine	Mercury
Cancer	Water	Cardinal	Feminine	Moon
Leo	Fire	Fixed	Masculine	Sun
Virgo	Earth	Mutable	Feminine	Mercury
Libra	Air	Cardinal	Masculine	Venus
Scorpio	Water	Fixed	Feminine	Mars/Pluto
Sagittarius	Fire	Mutable	Masculine	Jupiter
Capricorn	Earth	Cardinal	Feminine	Saturn
Aquarius	Air	Fixed	Masculine	Saturn/Uranus[4]
Pisces	Water	Mutable	Feminine	Jupiter/Neptune

[4] Uranus, Neptune and Pluto are planets in our Solar System that were discovered relatively recently. The correspondences of these 'new' planets are used by some modern astrologers. Where this is the case I have given both the modern and the original correspondence.

Table 6 shows the signs of the Zodiac in their correct order. A quick study will reveal a number of patterns. The elements are arranged against the signs sequentially through Fire, Earth, Air and Water. This may seem an unusual sequence at first, but it follows the sequence of physical creation. When the planet Earth was formed it was, at first, an extremely hot molten ball (fire). Once the planet began to cool we see Earth forming, followed by air, then water. The qualities associated with the signs alternate, as do the gender attributes. In doing so they create a natural gender balance that many consider essential in Wicca. Not only do the gender attributes alternate from one sign to the next, each of the three qualities of mutable, cardinal and fixed are associated with two masculine signs and two feminine.

Also note that this is where the gender attributes associated with the elements that are used in Wicca originate. Fire and Air are always masculine; Earth and Water are always feminine.

The Sun gradually moves through the twelve signs of the zodiac through the course of the Solar year. The zodiac begins with Aries, the starting point of which is determined by the Sun's position at the point of the spring equinox. Aries, therefore, represents new birth and those born under this sign often seem to possess a child-like need to explore and test everything, pushing buttons here, there, and everywhere in order to learn more about the self and how that self can affect others. By the time the Sun reaches Taurus those energies are beginning to become more grounded and there is a strong bullish sense of striding forwards through the growth process. People born under this influence often have a stubborn determination driving themselves through life. Taurus also brings the need to explore the material pleasures (being an earth sign) as well as the sensual (being ruled by Venus). Gemini brings a new perspective as the wheel turns and brings a realisation that there is more to life than the self and can be extremely transformative being a mutable sign.

By the time the Sun reaches Cancer, the new seeds have grown to become young plants heading towards full bloom. Cancer is a nurturing sign. The symbol used, the crab-like arms, can be viewed as the arms of a mother embracing a child. Cancer brings the need to understand the emotional and psychic relationships and to nurture those aspects in a creative fashion. Next up is Leo when the Sun is at its height and strongest. Leo is masculine fire and very much associated with the self and self-importance. Leo brings energies that often require those born under the sign to be the centre of attention. Leo can be generous and creative, but demands acknowledgement for what it gives. By the time the Sun reaches Virgo, however, this emphasis on the self has become tamed. Virgo is an earthy, mutable and feminine sign that starts to bring realisation that we are all an important part of a great collective. Those influenced by this sign will more likely find it easy to put the needs of others above those of the self in contrast to Leo.

This process is developed further in Libra, the sign of balance and harmony, where the importance of others, each with their own needs (emotional and mental) is fully appreciated. Scorpio brings with it a certain intensity. The Sun's cycle, mirroring that of humanity's development, has got to the point where it seeks a return to the source. Scorpio is a fixed water sign and associated with examining one's emotional and spiritual self-worth, as well as that of everyone else. It is a time when the lower ego can be transcended. What is the value of what has been gained through the Summer? In Wicca this is the theme of Samhain rituals as the season comes to its close. Sagittarius brings a new impetus on life: having transcended the ego in Scorpio it brings energies that encourage an exploration of the relationship to the big picture. The self is far less important to people influenced by this sign which is ruled by Jupiter, the planet associated with expansion, growth and freedom. Sagittarians can, however, be quite bullish and its arrow can represent a certain directness that hits its target without concern for the individual it hits as there is a certain element of not being able to see the trees for the wood!

As the Sun moves into Capricorn things become a little more grounded. With the year's seeds now fallen the foundation is laid for another year ahead. Capricorn brings a respect for the order of things and is ruthlessly concerned with integrity. Because of this, people with this influence can be hard-working and struggle to learn how to relax, often taking everything very seriously. Aquarius brings energies that build on the integrity and foundation that has been laid before it for the benefit of the group as a whole. Those influenced by Aquarius tend to love freedom and be terrific team players often with a utopian perspective. Finally Pisces completes the Solar cycle, helps to integrate everything that has been learned over that cycle together and corresponds with breaking through the illusion of being separated from the source. Pisces represents the final stage in the evolutionary process, a final ending. But as with all endings it simply leads to new beginnings as the Sun then moves back into Aries again.

THE PLANETS

The seven planetary bodies generally used by our pagan ancestors are the Sun, Moon, Mercury, Venus, Mars, Jupiter and Saturn. These are the

Table 7 – Symbols used for the planetary bodies

Planetary body	Symbol	Planetary body	Symbol
Sun	☉	Jupiter	♃
Moon	☾	Saturn	♄
Mercury	☿	Neptune	♆
Venus	♀	Uranus	♅
Mars	♂	Pluto	♇

only heavenly bodies, besides the stars, that are visible to the naked eye and, it would seem, the only ones our ancestors were consciously aware of. They are also the closest to the Earth and are therefore likely to have the strongest physical effect (though their energies don't *only* work on the physical plane).

We now know of several other planets within our Solar System – Neptune, Uranus and Pluto – as well as the fact that several of the planets also have moons of their own. (See Table 7 for the symbols used for planetary bodies.) These planets, discovered over the last two centuries, have largely been incorporated into modern astrology along with some of the larger asteroids that form part of the belt between Mars and Jupiter. There is evidence that some of our ancient ancestors did actually know about Neptune, Uranus and Pluto along with much other information about the physical Universe that has only been discovered (or rediscovered) in relatively recent years using high-tech equipment. *How* they know we may never know. Logic suggests that they either had access to high-tech equipment or had contact with species (or maybe even ancestors) from a far off planet, perhaps via the 'mythical' Atlantis. The jury is still out on that one though the truth is known on a deep level by all if one finds a way to delve far enough.

The seven planetary bodies that are incorporated into many of the symbols that have been handed down over the years do indeed have a profound effect on us that is worth understanding and working with. As pagans, from an Earthly perspective, we tend to focus a great deal of our attention on the Goddess in Her Earth and Moon aspects and the God in His Solar aspect and this is entirely reasonable as they have the most obvious and profound effect on us and we need to show them the respect they deserve for what they bring us. However, the energies of the divine work through the entire Cosmos, there are many

▲ *Figure 34 – The Hexagram*

gods and many goddesses. We should not dismiss the subtle energies coming from Neptune, Uranus, Pluto, the asteroids and any planets that astronomers have yet to discover, nor the energies coming through them from further afield for that matter. These are also important and also play a distinct role in our development even if we experience the energies only at a subtle level. Once we gain a better understanding of these energies we can gain a better understanding of ourselves and 'knowing oneself' is one of the great maxims of any form of esoteric path.

Perhaps the first symbol to look at is the six-pointed star, known by some as the Star of David, by others as the Seal of Solomon, and to pagans as the Hexagram (Figure 34).

The Hexagram is an important and useful symbol. It is sometimes referred to as the symbol of the macrocosm (pairing it with the Pentagram which is the symbol of the microcosm) because it can be seen to represent the heavenly bodies. The figure consists of two interlinked triangles. To a Wiccan this could be seen to represent the combined forces of the triple goddess within and without. The two triangles could also represent 'as above, so below'.

The Hexagram is a symbol that has been used by esotericists of many paths throughout the millennia. In alchemy, the metaphysical science of transformation (which is more correctly recognised as an inner spiritual transformation turning our symbolic base metal into gold) the Hexagram is used to derive the alchemical symbols used to represent Earth, Air, Fire and Water as shown in Figure 35. These symbols have been adopted by many Wiccans and those following other spiritual paths and fit in perfectly with the root influences of Wicca's founders (Table 8).

The planets are assigned positions on the points of the Hexagram with the Sun at its centre. The symbol has been adopted for use particularly by the Judaic faith which derived directly from a solar oriented spiritual path; the fact that the Sun is assigned the central position may well be a primary factor in this choice. The three planets outside of the Earth's

▲ *Figure 35 – The alchemical symbol for Earth in the Hexagram*

▲ *Figure 36 – The Planetary Bodies on the Hexagram*

Table 8 – Symbols used for the elements

Element	Earth	Air	Fire	Water
Symbol				

orbit are arranged on the points above the position of the Sun, those inside the Earth's orbit are as in Figure 36.

The five actual planets (i.e. excluding the Sun and Moon) are also assigned points on the sign on the Pentagram by the Golden Dawn (a

▲ *Figure 37 – The Planets on the Pentagram – according to the Golden Dawn*

▲ *Figure 38 – The Planets on the Pentagram – according to the author*

▲ *Figure 39 – The Elements on the Pentagram*

hermetic Christian tradition that heavily influenced Wicca) as in Figure 37. This arrangement does not work for me, though it may well be that the mixed elements were used by the Golden Dawn as a lesson or to hide the truth as was often the way. Spirit could not be represented by Saturn, in my opinion, as this planet represents the binding energies of the physical. Saturn could only work in this position if it were intended that it represented bringing the spiritual energies into the bounds on the physical plane. For me, Spirit would be better represented by Jupiter with its symbol representing the crescent of the soul moving into the cross of matter. The Golden Dawn have Mars representing Fire; this I could not disagree with as Mars could not go anywhere else. However, Venus (Goddess of love) is most definitely an emotional planet and doesn't work in the Earth position unless it is intended to invoke love on Earth (and a there is certainly a great need for that!). I would put Venus in the position representing Water and put Saturn in the Earth position instead. Mercury, which represents communication, would surely be better in the Air position above Earth (whilst appreciating the need to communicate the wisdom of Water). I would, therefore, end up with planetary correspondences with the Pentagram as in Figure 38.

John Dee, Queen Elizabeth I's well-known physician, is responsible for a whole system of hermetic Christian magic known as Enochian. Among the many symbols he derived was one that utilises a form of the seven-pointed star, representing the seven planetary influences, with a pentagram at its centre, representing the magician or human microcosm. John Dee's famous 'pentagram' is surrounded by Enochian code for the names of various hermetic Christian angels along with many other symbols. The central element of this 'pentagram', Figure 40, is quite an attractive one that could be used readily within Wiccan Circles, especially

▲ *Figure 40 – A seven-pointed star surrounding a pentagram – the central feature extrapolated from John Dee's famous 'pentagram'*

▲ *Figure 41 – A more elaborate version of Solomon's Seal with planetary and zodiacal symbolism*

if working with planetary energies. I use a version of this, as featured on the front cover of this volume to symbolise the path I have chosen to call Rainbow Wicca as mentioned earlier. This symbolism is very similar to a more elaborate version of the Seal of Solomon shown in Figure 41 which incorporates not only the seven planetary energies, but also the twelve zodiacal energies just as with Figure 30.

The planets also find their way onto the Tree of Life, as in Figure 42. Some of the reasoning behind this has been discussed in the chapter on the Tree. Keter does not have an attribute as it represents the first stirrings from the source. Chokmah represents the divine positive force and is therefore represented by the entire zodiac. Binah is associated with Saturn, the binding receptive force in the Solar system. Jupiter and Mars are associated with Chesed and Geburah respectively; these two planets are placed further away from the Earth than the Sun and are therefore behind the direction in which we generally face (beyond the liminal threshold). The Sun represents the beauty of Tifaret as has been discussed already. Venus and Mercury, the closest two planets to the Sun, are associated with Netzach and Hod respectively. Yesod is associated with the Moon and Malkut with Earth, for obvious reasons.

PLANETARY MAGICAL SQUARES

Planetary Squares, planetary tablets or 'magical squares' were developed in ancient times by those who recognised the link between numbers, geometry and the divine – a time before these disciplines were compartmentalised and

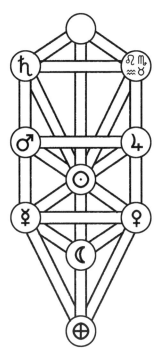

▲ *Figure 42 – Planets on the Tree of Life*

divided. They are fascinating for those with a mathematical mind and highly valuable for incorporating into ritual, talismans or seals when a particular planetary energy is deemed appropriate.

Each square is devised from the magical number associated with the planet and consists of the numbers from one to the square of that magical number arranged in a square. In each case each row, each column and each of the main diagonals add up to the same number and by adding up the total one can find further significances associated with each planet. For instance, the tablet for the Sun, whose magical number is 6, consists of a square 6 by 6 with numbers from 1 to 36. Each row or column adds up to 111 which when the 6 rows or columns are added together result in the number 666. This is the number of the Sun God that became demonised by those wishing to denigrate paganism in the early days of Christianity, but is held sacred for those with a nature-based spirituality. The tablet for the Moon, whose magical number is 9, has rows and columns adding up to 369. 369 when reduced numerologically $(3 + 6 + 9 = 18$, then $1 + 8 = 9)$ still ends up with a number whose square root is 3. In Wicca, and other pagan paths, the number 3 and multiplications of 3 (such as 9) relate to the triple Goddess aspects

6	32	3	34	35	1
7	11	27	28	8	30
19	14	16	15	23	24
18	20	22	21	17	13
25	29	10	9	26	12
36	5	33	4	2	31

▲ *Figure 43 – Magical Square of the Sun*

associated with the Moon. Furthermore, if those 9 columns, each adding up to 369, are added together they result in the number 3321. Again this can still be reduced numerologically to 9. It is a useful and educational exercise to study the other tablets, included in the pages following, for each of the planets.

SUN

The Sun sits in the centre of our planetary system and brings warmth, light and other energy to us on the physical plane. It is associated with the Sun God who brings the pure force that the Goddess utilises to create the wonderful bounty of form that exists in abundance all around us.

The Sun's energy is associated with authority, leadership, power, growth, vitality and success and can be used in rituals where such energies are appropriate. Its magical number is 6. Figure 43 shows the magical square for the Sun.

MOON

The Moon is the closest planetary body in the solar system to the Earth and reflects the light of the Sun in different aspects associated with Goddess in Her various guises affecting the tides and the emotional energies in subtle (and sometimes not so subtle) ways. The Moon is the Queen of the night sky.

The Moon's energy is associated with the emotions, with dreams, with astral travel, clairvoyance, the mysteries, fertility, reincarnation, and particularly with feminine issues. Its magical number is 9. Figure 44 shows the magical square for the Moon.

MARS

Mars is the nearest true planet to Earth whose passage lay outside of our own orbit in relation to the Sun. It is known and appears as the 'red

37	78	29	70	21	62	13	54	5
6	38	79	30	71	22	63	14	46
47	7	39	80	31	72	23	55	15
16	48	8	40	81	32	64	24	56
57	17	49	9	41	73	33	65	25
26	58	18	50	1	42	74	34	66
67	27	59	10	51	2	43	75	35
36	68	19	60	11	52	3	44	76
77	28	69	20	61	12	53	4	45

▲ *Figure 44 – Magical Square of the Moon*

planet'. Mars is known as the God of War and various other names with similar associations.

Mars energy brings much that is generally considered negative, such as war and other conflicts, anger, destruction, but with care it can be used positively in competition and struggle. Mars is not an easy energy to work with successfully and requires a sound balance. Its magical number is 5. Figure 45 shows the magical square for Mars.

MERCURY

Mercury is the nearest planet to the Sun and moves rapidly in its relatively small orbit. Being near to the Sun it is obviously a very hot and fiery planet and is known as the Messenger God bringing its message from the fiery heart of the divine.

Mercury's rapidity means it is often associated with matters that require action and its association with being a messenger relates it to communication. It is therefore often associated with business and trade – buying and selling, with memory, intellect, information and writing.

11	24	7	20	3
4	12	25	8	16
17	5	13	21	9
10	18	1	14	22
23	6	19	2	15

▲ *Figure 45 – Magical Square of Mars*

129

8	58	59	5	4	62	63	1
49	15	14	52	53	11	10	56
41	23	22	44	45	19	18	48
32	34	35	29	28	38	39	25
40	26	27	37	36	30	31	33
17	47	46	20	21	43	42	24
9	55	54	12	13	51	50	16
64	2	3	61	60	6	7	57

▲ *Figure 46 – Magical Square of Mercury*

Its magical number is 8. Figure 46 shows the magical square for Mercury.

JUPITER

Jupiter is the largest of the planets in our system and orbits outside of the asteroid belt that is associated with the liminal threshold. A large gaseous planet that appears blue from the Earth. The Romans knew Jupiter as the God of gods. In Wicca it is referred to in the Wiccan Rede as the 'blue star' that is worn on the brow.

Because it is a large gaseous planet, Jupiter is associated with expansion and spiritual growth, but also with light-hearted matters such as entertainment, parties, gambling and sometimes fortunes. Its magical number is 4. Figure 47 shows the magical square for Jupiter.

VENUS

Venus is the nearest planet to Earth that orbits inside our own. Because it is most often seen in the early hours it is known as the 'Morning Star' and its apparent passage around the Sun creates a perfect pentacle when plotted. Venus is the Goddess of Love and has strong feminine virtues.

4	14	15	1
9	7	6	12
5	11	10	8
16	2	3	13

▲ *Figure 47 – Magical Square of Jupiter*

22	47	16	41	10	35	4
5	23	48	17	42	11	29
30	6	24	49	18	36	12
13	31	7	25	43	19	37
38	14	32	1	26	44	20
21	39	8	33	2	27	45
46	15	40	9	34	3	28

▲ *Figure 48 – Magical Square of Venus*

As such, Venus is associated with love and pleasures of all kinds, with creativity, art, music and social affairs as well as specifically with feminine sexuality. Its magical number is 7. Figure 48 shows the magical square for Venus.

SATURN

Saturn's orbit lays beyond that of Jupiter and is the furthest planet from the Sun visible with the naked eye. It is best known for its beautiful rings that are symbolic of the binding and restrictive energies it represents.

Saturn is associated with limitations, obstructions, discipline and sometimes death. It is, however, also associated with structures and buildings, with institutions such as banks and debts. Its magical number is 3. Figure 49 shows the magical square for Saturn.

THE SEVEN-POINTED STAR AND PLANETARY TABLES

Figure 50 shows the seven major planetary bodies that our ancestors were aware of aligned to the seven-pointed star. Each of these planets is associated with a certain God or Goddess that lend their names to the days of the week as Table 9 shows. Because of the rich diversity of culture that has been involved in European development over the millennia, the names we have ended up with actually have their roots in a mixture of pagan traditions, mainly Anglo-Saxon and Roman.

4	9	2
3	5	7
8	1	6

▲ *Figure 49 – Magical Square of Saturn*

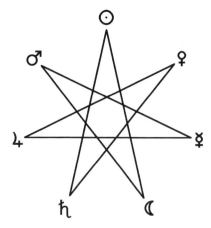

▲ *Figure 50 – The planets on the seven-pointed star*

Looking at Figure 50 you will notice that by starting at the upper-most point of the star (the Sun/Sunday) and following the way the star is draw in a clockwise direction, the planets match the days of the week in the correct order.

If we now number the planets around the star, working from the Sun deosil (clockwise) around the circumference we end up with a new sequence as in Figure 51.

The numerical sequence now gives us the Sun, Venus, Mercury, the Moon, Saturn, Jupiter, and Mars. This is the sequence used to derive the tables for the magical hours of the day in the Table of Planetary Hours. The Table of Planetary Hours (Table 10) has been used for many hundreds of years. Whilst its origins are unclear, the earliest record of it are found in The Key of Solomon (reputedly written around the 10th

Table 9 – Days of the week and goddesses and gods associated with the planets

Symbol	Planetary body	Day of week	Goddess/God
☉	Sun	Sunday	Sun (many names)
☾	Moon	Monday	Moon (many names)
♂	Mars	Tuesday	Tew (Saxon)
☿	Mercury	Wednesday	Wodin (Saxon)
♃	Jupiter	Thursday	Thor (Saxon)
♀	Venus	Friday	Freya (Saxon)
♄	Saturn	Saturday	Saturnalia (Roman)

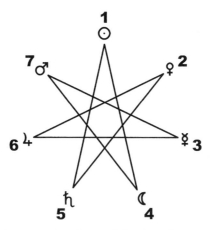

▲ *Figure 51 – The planets numbered around the circumference of the seven-pointed star*

century BCE. (Certain manuscripts still exist in the British Museum.) This table can be used to find the most appropriate planetary energies to utilise in any magical work. When used in conjunction with corresponding herbs, metals, colours, incense and symbolic devices, the magical work will gain considerable focus and strength.

By studying Table 9 you will notice that the planet that corresponds with the first hour following sunrise matches that of the day of the week (whichever day you choose). You will also notice that the planets associated with each hour follow the same sequence as that found by following the circumference on the seven-pointed star in Figure 51. The sequence is continuous throughout the whole table following on from one day to the next.

There are two ways to use the table, one more accurate than the other.

The first (and less accurate) method is to work out the hour from midnight using standard Greenwich Meantime (if in the UK). For instance, if you have decided that the most appropriate day to work on is a Monday and you also want to work with energies from Venus, then you have a number of choices. By running your finger down the Monday column until you find Venus, then move your finger to the left to the Hours from Midnight column, you find that the best times to work at would be 04.00, 11.00, or 18.00 hours.

The second, more accurate method, is to calculate the times of the sunrise and sunset. The only days of the year when the times between sunrise and sunset are equal are at the two equinoxes. A good ephemeris will provide the precise times for you. You then need to use a calculator

Table 10 – Table of the planetary hours

Hours from sunset/sunrise	Day or night	Hours from midnight	Sunday	Monday	Tuesday	Wednesday	Thursday	Friday	Saturday
8		1	Mercury	Jupiter	Venus	Saturn	Sun	Moon	Mars
9		2	Moon	Mars	Mercury	Jupiter	Venus	Saturn	Sun
10		3	Saturn	Sun	Moon	Mars	Mercury	Jupiter	Venus
11		4	Jupiter	Venus	Saturn	Sun	Moon	Mars	Mercury
12		5	Mars	Mercury	Jupiter	Venus	Saturn	Sun	Moon
1		6	Sun	Moon	Mars	Mercury	Jupiter	Venus	Saturn
2		7	Venus	Saturn	Sun	Moon	Mars	Mercury	Jupiter
3		8	Mercury	Jupiter	Venus	Saturn	Sun	Moon	Mars
4		9	Moon	Mars	Mercury	Jupiter	Venus	Saturn	Sun
5		10	Saturn	Sun	Moon	Mars	Mercury	Jupiter	Venus
6		11	Jupiter	Venus	Saturn	Sun	Moon	Mars	Mercury
7		12	Mars	Mercury	Jupiter	Venus	Saturn	Sun	Moon
8		13	Sun	Moon	Mars	Mercury	Jupiter	Venus	Saturn
9		14	Venus	Saturn	Sun	Moon	Mars	Mercury	Jupiter
10		15	Mercury	Jupiter	Venus	Saturn	Sun	Moon	Mars
11		16	Moon	Mars	Mercury	Jupiter	Venus	Saturn	Sun
12		17	Saturn	Sun	Moon	Mars	Mercury	Jupiter	Venus
1		18	Jupiter	Venus	Saturn	Sun	Moon	Mars	Mercury
2		19	Mars	Mercury	Jupiter	Venus	Saturn	Sun	Moon
3		20	Sun	Moon	Mars	Mercury	Jupiter	Venus	Saturn
4		21	Venus	Saturn	Sun	Moon	Mars	Mercury	Jupiter
5		22	Mercury	Jupiter	Venus	Saturn	Sun	Moon	Mars
6		23	Moon	Mars	Mercury	Jupiter	Venus	Saturn	Sun
7		24	Saturn	Sun	Moon	Mars	Mercury	Jupiter	Venus

(unless your mental arithmetic is particularly good) and divide the number of hours between sunrise and sunset, or sunset and sunrise (depending on the time you decide to work) into twelve equal parts. Then by translating that to the standard clock measurement you can work out the necessary correspondences.

Having done all of that, you can then proceed to other correspondences appropriate to those energies you have chosen by using further tables to pick colours, herbs, incense etc. Remember that preparation and planning are just as much part of any magical work as the ritual itself. As soon as you start to plan and prepare items, symbols, times, colours etc., you are already focusing on the work at hand and putting energy into it. This is time consuming indeed. Those who think they can simply buy a book of spells, cast a quick Circle, read out a few words, then step back to wait for results are likely to wait a long time. Working magic requires dedication, sincerity, knowledge and patience. An appropriate combination of these will bring results that are hard to break.

USING AN EPHEMERIS

There are a great many ephemeri on the market. For most purposes one of the simpler versions such as those found in some esoteric diaries are adequate. I tend to use Raphael's Ephemeris, which is available each year, is easy to read, but has more detail if you choose to delve deeper. There are some very good and easy to use computer-based versions that can be downloaded from the Internet.

An ephemeris will give you information of the exact movement of the planets against their background of the twelve signs of the zodiac. It will provide you with the precise times of transit for any event throughout the year including the most basic – that of the Sun and Moon. This means, for those of you who like precision like me, you will be able to see exactly when the Sun moves from one zodiacal sign to the next and thus the ideal time to perform celebrations or rituals. You will also have a chart telling you the precise moment of the full Moon and Her other aspectations. The charts give the position of all these celestial movements as if the Earth were a stationary object around which everything else moves, which is of course false, but a natural and easier to conceive perspective than the actuality. Even so, the ephemeris still gives us information about any planets position in relation to the Earth, which is the point of interest and relevance.

If you happened to be working on improving your communication skills, or have a need to communicate a complex matter to a friend or colleague, you might want to choose a time when the planet associated with communication (Mercury) is in your Sun sign (or if needing to communicate about a matter more closely associated with emotional matters in your Moon sign). An ephemeris will provide you with the data to determine the ideal time for such communication.

You may notice that in many of these emphemeri there is a reference to 'siderial time'. Siderial time is slightly different to the time as determined normally by our 24-hour clock. The normal clock divides a day into 24 equal parts as determined by the rotation of the Earth that we witness by the rise and setting of the Sun. Siderial time is stellar time, rather than earth time. The sidereal clock divides a day into 24 equal parts as determined by the position of Aries. Because the Earth is both rotating on its own axis as well as rotating around the Sun, the Earth's position in relation to Aries is slightly different at the end of each day and because of this the sidereal 'day' is just over a minute longer than what we consider to be a normal 24 hours. For general purposes, even if you like to be accurate, this is such a small difference that it isn't worth worrying about, though it is useful to have an understanding of the difference.

9

MEDITATION AND TRANCE

The daily discipline of meditation is common to most, if not all, esoteric spiritual paths. Wicca and witchcraft are no exceptions. I included a section on meditation in my first book *Wiccan Spirituality* and include a further elaboration in this volume in an effort to emphasise what I consider to be the fundamental importance of establishing a disciplined meditation regime.

Meditation is an exceptionally good way of relaxing the lower mind and keeping grounded. However, relaxation is only the initial benefit from meditation. Once a simple technique is perfected, then one can enter the astral planes and the mental planes to undertake your work. As a witch your contact with your Higher Self, your guides, guardians and the goddesses and gods themselves, comes through from the spiritual realms. It is, most often, necessary to meet them half way by moving through the astral levels at least to the mental plane. If you do not regularly meditate, then your ability to work with these entities will be severely limited, and your role as a witch will most likely be limited to that of fantasy and glamour! Even the most adept and hard working High Priestesses and High Priests need to keep up this discipline, in fact they need to do even more work usually as the tightrope does not become easier to tread, it just gets narrower and higher.

The discipline of meditation leads on to one of the most important skills for anyone who intends to work magic – that of visualisation. The ability to obtain a strong visualisation and (most importantly) maintain it, is the key to bringing energy from the higher mental plane, through the emotional plane, then into physical manifestation. If one is in touch with the spiritual, which is the objective for any Wiccan, then the work of magic will have begun from even higher planes and this is a major discipline that will enable you to develop a true and valuable service to the Goddess and God.

If your meditation regime has fallen by the wayside, do not despair. There are times when the best of us need a rest. But do your best to get back into the routine as soon as you can. Meditation is one of the most effective ways of maintaining the balance that is essential for any form of spiritual development work. It is far more than a way of relaxation. Through meditation we train ourselves to be able to break down the barriers between the planes and open channels of communication that turn on the tap of energy that we need to bring from those planes into physical if we are to make the most of our calling to be an effective witch.

Remember always that the ability to meditate is necessary in order to do a great deal of energy work. The ability to visualise, a key skill when it comes to working real magic, comes with practice through your meditations, and this is also a key skill that needs to be developed. Remember also, that there is an important difference between meditation and trance. In a meditation you set the conscious mind to one side, but can re-enter it at will and with little effort. In trance we are entirely letting go of the conscious mind, and this skill needs to be developed with care and (ideally) with others present. Trance work will be discussed in more detail later in this chapter.

LEARNING TO MEDITATE

Meditation can be a very relaxing exercise, but as you develop you will also discover that eventually it is the time you get to spend in contact with your Higher Self, your guides and many other energies that are an essential part of living and working as a witch.

A disciplined and daily routine of meditation is an essential element to spiritual growth. This is something that many will find difficult to fit into the modern hectic lifestyle, though paradoxically something that will infinitely help us cope with it too. It is the connection made through the subconscious during meditation that we begin to discover our Higher Selves. ('Higher self' can also be described as the 'inner self', 'spiritual consciousness', 'super conscious', creative force' and many other names. Whatever term is used it is basically the same, though the super conscious is more correctly applied to the fully opened channel to the whole soul, rather than an element of it.) It is through this discovery that we find the key to unlock the boundaries between the physical plane and the other planes that at first remain unseen but are part of the key to future magical work. It is our link to that which takes care of our spiritual well-being and retains our 'universal memory'. Meditation opens the door to personal spiritual growth, psychic development and all that there is beyond what we perceive as the extremely limited reality in our normal everyday lives.

Meditation comes easier to some than others, though everyone can do it and get better at it with practice. There are many forms of meditation and many methods are taught, none particularly more or less valid than any others, although some techniques will suit us better as individuals than others. Many techniques have their roots in eastern traditions but are often easily adapted for use in any spiritual path.

At first it would be best to simply use meditation purely for relaxing, clearing one's mind of the day to day clutter of modern living and using it to visualise a clear and empty space. Once this has been achieved one can go with the flow of any images that come up of their own accord. Meditation can be used to focus on issues and, once a technique is fully developed, can lead onto contemplation through which comes a new and clear connection, through one's higher self.

Some techniques employ the use of a mantra that is chanted. This may be of some use for those who have trouble learning how to meditate, and is a way of shutting out the conscious mind and the chatter that often accompanies it. By focusing on a mantra you are, however, not fully allowing the space for the subconscious thought forms to flow so I feel the use of such techniques has limitations.

During meditation the brain enters an altered state of consciousness – known as 'alpha' – a state also entered during deep relaxation and dreaming. In the alpha state the brain waves register at between seven and fourteen cycles. This is close to the background energy cycles of the Earth itself. (When mentally alert the brain registers at fourteen to thirty cycles per second – known as Beta. The slower rate of four to seven cycles per second, associated with drowsiness and euphoria, is known as Theta, whilst the Delta state of deep dreamless sleep works at one to three cycles per second.)

Through practice, work in the alpha state can open one up to a whole new, much broader, sense of reality than hitherto discovered. Not only can one benefit enormously from temporarily by-passing the glamours (self-delusions) of the ego to gain contact and communication with one's higher self, but one is also better able to develop skills such as telepathy, clairvoyance and pre-cognition. It is in the alpha state that we are able to enter and explore the other planes of reality that include the astral and spiritual planes creating a situation where we are much more open and receptive to the energies that exist all around us, rather than just those on the more commonly recognised physical plane. A regular routine is important in order to benefit fully as the effects are cumulative. Alpha is a state where we can expand into the vibrationary rates of the other planes of existence. It is whilst working between these planes where much of the occult work is undertaken – which will be discussed more fully in future lessons.

Meditation is basically the means by which we gain access to the quantum reality; a greater sense of the breadth of reality than we are commonly aware of as a young adolescent, or even as an adult if we haven't explored beyond the materialistic physical plane. Visualisation work during meditation is a vital element in magic whether it be used, as many do, for healing purposes or other intentions.

Having mastered basic meditation techniques, the next step is to start working on visualisations. Starting with simple objects such as a burning candle, or an apple, one can gradually start building up quite complex images. Once mastered, one can continue to use meditation as a door to the astral plane that can be used for all sorts of work including building your own personal temple that can become your own private and personal space. This will be discussed in more detail in a later volume.

The first thing to do when preparing to meditate is find a suitable location. If it is warm and sunny, and you have access to the countryside, or even a decent park, sitting under a tree or among flowers can be very invigorating (though it is important to find somewhere you can be in private and will not be disturbed). At home, finding a quiet place to sit, either in a comfortable chair, or on the floor is ideal. Sitting in front of your altar can be quite inspiring. It is important that you are not going to be disturbed, so take the phone off the hook, turn any mobile phones off too, and if you share the house with others let them know what you are doing and that you would appreciate it if you are not disturbed. Having a phone ring, or a child shout in your ear once deep in meditation can be quite disturbing to say the least.

Make sure that you sit comfortably. Many people like to sit crossed-legged or in a lotus position (as in Eastern techniques) but this is far from essential. The important thing is that you are comfortable, and that you sit upright with your spine straight so that the energies can flow through your body uninhibited; the posture is very important as it helps us to breathe properly and breath control is a key element in most techniques. If sitting in a chair it is good to use an upright chair with a high back. If sitting on the floor it is a good idea to use a cushion or two under your bottom. You can meditate laying flat on your back if you prefer, though this may lead to you fall asleep which is not entirely desirable and therefore not recommended.

DISTRACTING THE CONSCIOUS MIND

Many people of a more active nature experience difficulty training the conscious mind to let go. The conscious mind loves to be 'in control' and will try all sorts of things to keep things that way including reminding you about a relatively unimportant phone call, or the need to put the rubbish bins out (when in fact another hour is soon enough). If you do have problems meditating because the conscious mind keeps kicking in then you can use various techniques in order to occupy its attention while you spend twenty minutes with your subconscious. Different techniques will suit different people, but they are all essentially ways of creating something mundane to attract the conscious mind's attention while you go off in a different plane for a while. They can involve utilising the senses of sound or vision.

METHOD ONE

Drumming is a technique often utilised for this purpose by those who follow a shamanic path. The regular beat offers a distraction to the conscious mind, whilst the vibration attracts the attention of the spirits that the shaman is intending to communicate with. This is a technique you may want to try, though meditation is not necessarily about communicating with spirit, and a practising shaman will tend to continue this process beyond the realms of meditation and into trance where even the subconscious is being transcended.

METHOD TWO

Another technique involves using music. You need to pick a gentle piece of music, one without words (the words will offer visual suggestion). The new age style of music that rambles on at a gentle pace without too many peaks is ideal for this. You will need to make all the usual preparations for meditation and put the music on very quietly, in fact barely audible. This will give something for your conscious mind to focus in on. If you find them comfortable, using a pair of headphones can help this process with the added advantage of cutting out some background noises.

METHOD THREE

This technique uses vision rather than sound to offer a distraction. Copy Figure 52 onto a white piece of card using the same dimensions and thickness of lines as used here. Darken the room as much as possible and prop

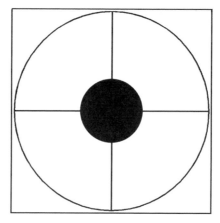

▲ *Figure 52 – A tool for aiding meditation*

the card up at just below eye level a few feet in front of where you are able to sit comfortably. A coffee table is ideal for this, though you need to ensure that the rest of the coffee table is empty, you do not need other distractions nearby. Place a candle about at foot in front of the propped-up card between it and where you will be sitting and slightly to the right, you want to be able to see clearly past the candle. Ensure the candle is lit then sit down and meditate as normal, but with your eyes open and firmly focused on the black dot in the centre of the drawing. If your eyes begin to drift away from the dot, just bring your focus back to it as soon as you notice. Continue to focus on the dot.

The first time I tried this I saw smoke drifting out of the centre of the dot for several minutes and went into a deep meditation, even though I was suffering with a very painful broken arm at the time. It can be a very powerful technique. If at any time you find yourself drifting off and your eye lids feel so heavy you feel the need to close them, do so. Your subconscious will have taken over and you will come back into full consciousness before long.

RELEASING TENSION AND ACHIEVING EMOTIONAL BALANCE

Meditation reduces stress and tension on all levels. It is this tension, physical, emotional and mental, that creates blockages that hinder our development. Not until we learn how to releases these tensions properly will we be able to fully benefit from the energy from the spiritual plane.

Be aware that this process is not necessarily an entirely smooth one. Tension can be the result of unresolved issues (and we all have many of them even after several years of work) and is therefore a protective mechanism. You need to deal with the issues rather than try to by-pass them. An attempt to by-pass will not gain the results you may crave, but send you down a blind alley that leads to self-delusion and fantasy. (Fantasy being a way of avoiding reality.) Tensions build up in the physical body, often without you realising it. These tensions create blockages of energy flow through your entire system and on all levels. If you do not take the time to release these tensions, and thereby liberate the energy flow, then serious problems can arise. The nature of such problems will depend on where the tensions are located and how they interact with each other, but a dysfunction manifesting as a physical, emotional or mental symptom, may well have its root cause elsewhere. Regular meditation will tend to guard against any major build ups of tension under normal circumstances; however, you may well be surprised how easily small pockets can escape attention. The following meditation can be a valuable one to run through from time to time as a double check (and most people will find some pockets of tension, no matter how disciplined the meditation regime). It can be of particular value following a time when you may have experienced exceptional physical, emotional or mental pressure (such as following an accident, etc).

It has been proven in medical experiments[5] that meditation reduces stress and thereby helps any healing process, though it need not be employed simply when serious healing is required. Everyday life in the 21st century provides more than enough stress to warrant a regular routine simply on health grounds. Hospital patients, after having been given lessons over an eight week period, were found to have increased electrical activity on the left side of the frontal lobe, a region thought to be linked to lowering anxiety and stimulating a more positive emotional state.

The following meditation will help release tension throughout the body even when you may feel that you have little in the way of tension (you'll be surprised what you find).

Do all the normal preparations for a meditation, such as ensuring the phone is switched off. Light some incense. Sit comfortably either with your legs crossed, or in a high-backed chair. The important thing is that you are comfortable and that your back is straight.

---

[5] Department of Complementary Medicine at the University of Exeter 2003, for instance.

If you can record the following words at a slow comfortable pace, you may find this even move effective. If you do so, then read it slowly, with plenty at breaks at appropriate places and try to use a fairly steady tone rather than use emotive language – the sub-conscious reacts better to a more monotonous tone, the conscious attempts to kick in when it hears emotion in order to analyse it.

Allow your mind to settle. Close your eyes and take three long deep breaths through your nostrils filling your lungs fully and holding for a few seconds between each in and out function. Then just sit quietly and allow your breathing to settle into a normal and gentle rhythm.

When you are ready, begin to visualise a small ball of intense light hovering just above the crown of your head. Hold the visualisation until it is steady and strong. Then bring this energy down slowly into your head and across your brow. As it passes over each muscle, notice the tension in that area just soften and melt away. Take your time – there is no rush!

Move the energy around part of your face – around the sides of your eyes, the length of your nose, your cheeks, your mouth and lips etc. Everywhere it passes, feel the muscles soften and relax – feel the tension just drop away.

Now continue to work down from your head into your neck, everywhere the ball of light touches simply softens and relaxes. Then across one of your shoulders, to the top of your arm, down the length of your arm, to your wrist and hands. Everywhere the light touches instantly softens and the tension drops away. Run down the length of each finger and the thumb. Then go back to your shoulders and work your way down the other arm in the same way. Remember not to miss a single muscle and not to hurry.

When both arms are feeling light and completely free of tension, move the ball of energy to your throat and gradually down the front of your body, around your breasts, your abdomen, your stomach and right down to your genital area. Everywhere it touches just softens and relaxes.

Next take the energy back to the rear of your neck and slowly work down the length at your spine. Take extra time when you get to your buttocks, feeling the light energy release all the tension before you allow it to work down the length of each leg, down to the heel, the arch of your foot, right down to your toes.

When you get to your toes, allow all the excess energy that the ball of light has washed from your body to flow harmlessly into the Earth. The Earth Goddess will transform the energy for you, but take the time to thank Her.

Now your entire body is totally relaxed. Finish the exercise with some nice deep breaths. As you do so, visualise your whole body generating a soft gentle glow of pure health and harmony.

In your own time, bring yourself back to your room. Blessed be.

TRANCE

The experience of trance work needs to be approached with more caution. With normal meditation you are always maintaining a certain level of conscious control. You are distracting the conscious mind so that you can delve into the sub-conscious for a while but always maintain the ability to refocus and bring yourself back. With trance you are, to one degree or another, letting go of conscious control. This, as you can probably imagine, is not something to try without experienced guidance and with supervision.

Through trance techniques it is entirely possible to open your own mental vehicle up for use by a disincarnate spirit. This could be a guide or just simply someone who has passed on. The considerations for this are discussed more fully in the next chapter. In some techniques you 'instruct' your conscious mind to let go for a short time in order to enter the trance state and for it to 'bring you back' and regain conscious control at a predefined point. In other techniques you submit this guidance to a trusted and experienced colleague to whom you submit your will entirely. This, as you can imagine, requires a great deal of trust and integrity. If undertaken properly you can be submitting your will to some powerful energies and entities. It is *not* a game so do not play!

10

OF SPIRITS, GUIDES, ANGELS AND DEMONS

MEDIUMSHIP AND SPIRITUALISM

The art of mediumship is one that is much misunderstood and open to fraudulent misuse. It is a range of methods used to communicate with the spirits of souls that are no longer in an incarnate condition. It is also a matter on which spiritualists and occultists often disagree for very important and fundamental reasons. This is something that deserves serious consideration and requires a reasonable understanding of the process of life, dealt and rebirth, as well as an appreciation of the difference between body, spirit and soul.

When a physical body dies its soul goes through a process of splitting away from the material remains that bound its spirit to the physical plane. During the process, its separation from the physical body can be very sudden, as in the case of a serious car accident, or it can be comparatively slow as in the case of dying from a disease such as cancer. In both cases the process can be extremely disorientating. It has to get used to a new form of existence, or rather one with which it has become unfamiliar. In the case of sudden death this is particularly disorientating and can lead to a situation of denial. In the case of a slower death the individual has time whilst still in an incarnate state of getting used to the idea of dying even giving some consideration to what lay ahead.

Once the physical part of the body has dropped away and entered a state of decay, the lower emotional part then begins to break away and decays as well with it. No lower emotional attachment should remain but can if it is fed by enough emotional energy, as unhelpful as this may be. Using the model of the Four Trees discussed earlier in this volume it is possible to obtain a diagrammatic understanding of this (see Figure 53). In this diagram you should be able to see how the planes overlap. The emotional plane begins at the Tifaret of the physical

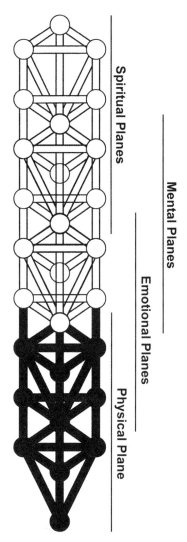

▲ *Figure 53 – At 'death' the Physical drops away and decays and takes with it the Lower Emotional with it*

plane. The lower emotional element is therefore that part which falls below the Tifaret of the emotional plane. Because the lower emotional element of the emotional plane overlaps with the physical and the higher emotional does not, the lower emotional element begins to decay (if it is not prevented) once the physical plane elements has dropped away as denoted by the grey area in the figure. Note also that the mental plane overlaps the upper part of the emotional that is retained allowing for mental recall of the lower emotional plane as and when it may be required.

In an ideal situation, the spirit will find its way without too many problems to a 'place' (for want of a better term) that many pagans call 'the Summerland'. (In Eastern terminology it is identified as 'Devachan'.) It is a place where the experiences of the most recent life can be fully and objectively reviewed, where those experiences can be assimilated with these from previous lives, and where the next set of potential experiences can be considered. If the emotional body had not decayed, this objectivity would understandably be impossible. This is all undertaken with the benefit of full access to the Soul's full range of experiences, and in collaboration with one's spiritual guides and other members of the individual soul group. (The soul group consists of others with whom we regularly enter into incarnations with often undertaking different roles.) It is not possible to divulge how long this process actually takes as the entire concept of time is all a part of the illusion of the physical plane. Time – past, present and future – are in fact all part of one experience on the spiritual planes.

What has been described above is the normal process, but the transition between the physical plane and the Summerland is not always a smooth and easy one. Just as during an incarnation, it is the emotional (or astral) pasts that cause the greatest problems.

In the case of a sudden death, especially one involving violence of some kind, the anger (being an emotion) is so strong that progress is hindered. In cases such as this, help may be required from an understanding soul on the physical plane to help the trapped soul to overcome the confusion and move forwards and let go. However, it is not only the emotions of the soul that has left the physical plane that can prevent unfettered progress. The emotional attachment of those who lived that person, can act like a magnet and pull the deceased back towards the physical, leaving the soul trapped and confused.

It is for this reason that it is important that those left grieving a loss must let go, not just for their own sakes, but to enable the departed to make the safe passage across the waters (that represent the emotional plane) to the Summerland.

Having an understanding of this process, having developed a sensitivity to potential trapped contacts, and being a Wiccan priestess or priest, one may occasionally be called on to help. The call can come either from someone still living and grieving, or from a trapped soul.

Now we should be able to go back and consider the problems caused by some Spiritualists. (I would point out here that this most certainly does not apply to all Spiritualists.) Many of these well-meaning people spend a great deal of their time contacting the souls of the recently departed in order to either help comfort those who are grieving, or simply as a form of entertainment. Whilst this may well help to prove to the living that there is existence after death, one risks creating an emotional pull back towards the physical plane and thus preventing progress. That, in my opinion and that of other occultists is a matter of great irresponsibility despite the good intentions. It is surely the task of anyone who fully appreciates the process to offer help wherever possible, not hindrance.

Proper consideration also needs to be applied to the ceremony held to mark the passing over of an individual. If done well, such a ceremony can do a great deal to ease the process both for those still living, and for the departed. However, it not handled with care the opposite can be the case. It is a great responsibility.

HANDLING A TRAPPED SOUL

There are a number of different ways of handling the situation of a trapped soul – one that has, for whatever reason, been unable to let the emotional body decay after the death of the physical body.

The first thing you will need to do is to ascertain exactly what it is that you are dealing with. In many circumstances what is imagined as the trapped spirit of a soul, what is commonly referred to as a ghost, is actually nothing of the sort. It is very often the imagined contact of an emotionally unstable individual who needs help of another kind. It is also worth bearing in mind that what is being complained about is a spiritual guide who is doing their best to make contact. You need to investigate thoroughly before taking action. A fool rushes in where angels fear to tread!

The first thing to do is to talk at length to the person reporting the 'disturbance'. If you are convinced that the contact is real, you then need to attempt to make contact yourself in order to ascertain the best plan of action. There are a number of ways of doing this. Presuming you have developed a solid contact with your own guide or guides, you would do well to take their advice. Alternatively you can put yourself into a deep meditative state and simply try talking to the contact on the astral plane (as this is its most likely location).

There is no reason to 'fear' talking to spirit. Fear belongs to the emotional plane and if you approach the subject with fear in your heart then you either block the whole possibility of contact, or at best, misinterpret the messages and feelings coming through to you. This is where the importance of mental development comes in; with a reasonable understanding on the process of life and death, and the issues surrounding spirit, then one can easily overcome the fear as this tends to spring from the unknown. If you are familiar with the concept and accept its reality then you will know there is nothing to fear.

You also need to bear in mind this is NOT a game. By all means undertake this work when you need to, but do not attempt it for the purposes of entertainment or to impress those around you with your skills. You will only be doing yourself harm, as well as preventing the spirits from doing what they need to do. Those who 'play' with things such as ouija boards should not be surprised if spirits start 'playing' back. Those spirits are unlikely to be particularly evolved and can play some pretty rotten games. Just because they have passed on doesn't mean that they have any greater knowledge or higher ethical values. As they know the rules better than those who choose to 'play' they will almost certainly end up the winners in the 'game' and have the last laugh at your expense! There is nothing inherently 'evil' in a ouija board, it is a perfectly reasonable tool to use if used properly; people are often put off from stories from those who have used them for frivolous purposes and they only have themselves to blame.

Be prepared to receive quite a strong reaction as the contact may jump on you in great relief that someone is listening and responding properly at last! Try to be understanding of the contact's situation. Bear in mind that it may be in a very confused and frustrated condition. Ask the contact who they are and what has happened. Be kind, loving and patient. By this stage you should easily have worked out whether the contact is a spirit guide, a trapped soul, or some other kind of entity. When talking to the spirit, it is best to talk to them quite plainly using everyday language; there is no need to adopt a strange and mysterious tone to your voice as some seem to do.

In the case of a trapped soul you simply need to gently explain what has happened and encourage them to let go and move towards the light. They will understand as they will have seen this light and felt a pull towards it but had resisted, probably several times. You can assure them that there will be familiar and friendly souls there to greet them.

If the contact does happen to be a spirit guide, you may well be able to assist by passing on a message as appropriate.

If you are certain that the spirit you have contacted is trapped and needs to move on, and conversing with it does not work, then you may need to cast a Circle with the spirit inside it to break down the boundaries between the planes. Cast your Circle in the normal way.

When you are ready, invite the spirit to enter your Circle and ensure that it is at ease. You can then either go into a deep visualisation and use the following imagery.

You are standing by a large lake, the Moon shines bright towards the west above the water that is shrouded in mist ... Breathe in the cool night air ... There is no sound but the sound of darkness ... After a short while a small boat drifts towards you appearing out of the mist and comes to rest invitingly in front of you ... Turn around and invite the spirit to enter the boat with you ... the spirit steps on board and you get on to sit at the back ... assure the spirit that you are going to take it safely across the water to where friends are waiting ... The boat gently and slowly glides away from the shore and heads west towards the Moon hanging low above the water and now showing a gleaming silver trail ... your boat follows ... the mist begins to lift ... After a while you see land approaching ... It is an island that rises up out of the water ... There is a tall hill in the middle of this island, and there is the distant sound of drums and voices singing merrily ... This is Annwn, where spirits rest and recuperate after their journey through the land of form ... The boat gently comes to rest on the shore of the island ... you stay on board, but invite the spirit to step ashore and assure him/her that friends are waiting just ahead ... the spirit moves off and you wave farewell as the boat glides away back to where you came from.

Ensure that you are thoroughly grounded at the end of this and that you banish the quarters thoroughly. Once the Circle has been cleared, cleansing it thoroughly with a pleasant incense would help significantly.

If for any reason you are unable to make contact, whether it is because there is none, or because of some resistance you cannot overcome, please just tell the person you are working for the truth. Many a situation has been made worse by practitioners making something up because something has been expected by the person they are working for!

SPIRIT GUIDES

Whether we are aware of them or not, each person during an incarnation is assigned, or has chosen, a spiritual guide that is working from the spiritual plane to help us successfully complete the objectives and lessons we intended for ourselves whilst on the physical plane. They do not necessarily intervene all of the time: the bulk of the time we are left to just get on with the mundane, but whenever a crucial situation is entered they are there.

How successful they are at communicating with our lower minds will depend on our stage of development. For a person who has not progressed far from a spiritual perspective, the communication is far from assured. Such a person may well receive some guidance, and it would most likely enter their minds in the form of an idea that has been subtly planted there, but even if this is so there is no guarantee that the person will act on the advice. The emotional plane creates a dense barrier that clouds the signals. For those who have been through many incarnations and have learned to see through the fog, the communication can be sensed with greater clarity and that person may even experience what appears to be actual verbal communication (clairaudience) which may be combined with, to some degree or another, the feeling of being pushed (clairsentience). This feeling of being pushed can become very strong, to the point of nearly being knocked off of one's feet or shoved out of one's bed.

It is worth pointing out here that relatively advanced spiritual development is not synonymous with a well developed IQ. Advanced souls may well choose to experience life with a low IQ in order to learn specific lessons and less advanced souls may well choose an incarnation that has a high IQ for the same reasons.

Some people may have more than one spiritual guide. Some may even experience a hierarchy of guides, that is, some guides who appear to be on call whenever the situation demands, and other more advanced guides with great power and wisdom who appear infrequently.

Spiritual guides tend to be souls that have been through a considerable number of incarnations themselves and have taken on the role of being a teacher. The process of teaching is part of the growth experience. They may still have further incarnations to undertake, or they may progress along the teaching path to have a number of junior guides under their guidance. Once they have reached this level then they may well look in on one of their junior guide's charges, especially when crucial stages have been reached. Ultimately, in this hierarchy, each group of guides, headed by a senior guide, comes under the guidance of a master who steers the development of vast cultural groups of souls. There may be times, most likely extremely few and far between, that these masters will communicate with an individual incarnation to check on progress or to steer in a specific direction. If this happens to you there will be no doubt at all regarding the communication, it will be crystal clear and unmistakable.

For those of a sceptical disposition it is very easy to shut out and put barriers up against communication with their guides. If there is a lack of understanding, an inability to accept the possibility of anything real that cannot be proven as material through scientific experiment, then this is an effective barrier, and part of the growth process is in breaking down such barriers. Those who are more open to feeling will find it easier and more natural to accept communication. Air types, who survive on logic, will find the process more challenging. In either case, reading the wisdom of others will help break down any barriers, especially for the logical types, as this will offer scope for understanding and leave the lower mind more open to the possibility of reality that is less tangible than perhaps they had come to experience.

EXERCISE – MEETING YOUR SPIRIT GUIDE

This is a guided meditation. If you can record the following words at a slow comfortable pace, you may find this even more effective. If you do so, then read it slowly, with plenty at breaks at appropriate places and try to use a fairly steady tone rather than use emotive language – the sub-conscious reacts better to a more monotonous tone, the conscious attempts to kick in when it hears emotion in the voice in order to analyse it.

First of all, ensure you are perfectly comfortable . . . When you are ready you are going to close your eyes and take three deep breaths . . . Breathing in, fill your lungs with air, continue breathing in until you can breathe in no more . . . hold the breath for a moment, then breathe out slowly and completely . . . Breathe in again, breathing in deep . . . hold for a moment . . . then breathe out again . . . hold for a moment, then breathe in again deeply, breathing in a pure bright light that fills your entire body . . . as you breathe out, let any dark residues empty out with the breath . . . now, just let your breathing settle down to a gentle relaxed rhythm . . . breathing in . . . and out . . . in . . . and out.

You are walking down a wide path in a green forest . . . there are trees all around you . . . you hear the sounds of birds singing, bees busying themselves . . . the air is clear and fresh . . . continue walking along the path through the trees . . . the Sun shines through the leaves onto the forest floor in shafts of bright white light illuminating everything it touches . . . After a while, as you continue to walk forwards, the path starts to get a little narrower, the trees become a little denser . . . off to your right there is another, smaller path that leads off into the trees . . . take this path and continue walking . . . as you enter into trees it gets even denser, becomes darker, the canopy of the trees blocks out the light . . . ahead, in the gloom, the trees suddenly open into a little glade . . . tall branches arch over this glade above . . . as you enter there is a log in the centre laying on its side . . . you move towards it and sit down . . . After a short while you sense that you are no longer alone . . . there is someone else here, but this presence feels entirely comfortable and friendly ... there is a sense of great peace and harmony ... As if from nowhere this presence reveals itself, as if from the trees themselves, and moves towards you ... you remain seated and great your guide with a welcome smile ... you sit together for a while and just talk ...

You can ask anything of your guide ... take your time ... if any object is offered you then feel free to take it and offer thanks ... when you are ready stand up ... gently bow towards your guide and offer thanks ... you can return here anytime you like, whether it is for further guidance, or simply to relax ... you turn your back and move towards the path that brought you here ... You look back one last time into the glade, but it is empty again, except for the log laying in the centre ... your guide has drifted back into the gloom of the trees to await your call when needed ...

Head back along the narrow path until it rejoins the larger path ... the trees gradually open up again ... as you continue walking the way you came in you begin to notice once again the sound of the birds singing and the bees buzzing ... you see the glorious sunshine bring shafts of bright light through the trees ... when you get back to where you started ... take three nice long deep breathes ... in your own time, bring yourself back to the world of form ... stretch your fingers and toes ... and open your eyes ... Blessed be!

After any work like this it is useful to make notes in your journal. If you were given any objects by your guide, make a note of this, even if at the present time its meaning isn't entirely clear, it will be sometime in the future. Having kept a written record you will be able to recall the wisdom that has been shared with you more readily.

Your guide or guides (some people have more than one) are with you all the time. This does not mean that things will not happen to you that you find unpleasant, far from it, but they will be there to help you learn from such important lessons if only you care to listen. Remember, that to fully appreciate the good things in life it is often necessary to experience the negative, and in order to be able to help others through negative issues or events the best way is often to have been through them yourself. Karma is the full range of life experiences that you have gathered over many lives, the more experience you have the more resources you have to call on. Try to look for the positive lessons to be learned, even in the most dreadful situations. If you look hard enough you will be able to find them.

ANGELS AND DEMONS

The term 'angel' is one that I generally associate with Christianity. The word conjures up images, to me at least, of smiling luminous humanoid creatures floating several feet off the ground with halos and wings. It is quite possible that spirit guides will appear to you in this way if this is how you expect to see them, though for me they tend to come to me in a somewhat more grounded form. As has been discussed in the previous few paragraphs, everyone has a spirit guide, or a number of spirit guides. What are commonly known as angels are usually these very same spirit guides, and they will tend to appear to you, if indeed they present themselves in visual form, in whatever way you expect to see them. Their actual form is not of the physical plane – they consist of an energy vibrating far beyond the physical plane that can become visible as a brilliant aura type of 'light'. I prefer to refer to these entities simply as spirit guides, they do not seem to mind what we call them.

There is a complex hierarchy of spirit guides. There are those which are assigned to individual incarnations, those who are more advanced and look after a group of spirit guides, there are those that are guiding the development of a whole range of cultural groups, each in different ways, and there are even those guiding the development of nations and doing their best to find ways of drawing all these nations together. When you meet these entities you will do well to listen, especially if you are visited by one of the higher forms.

Demons, on the other hand, are something that come in many shapes and sizes and are often misunderstood. Demons could refer to the shadow self that is within all of us. For those who have not incorporated the shadow self into their everyday lives can find that this 'daemon' finds its way to the surface from time to time and does things that appear to confuse us and which seem totally out of character. We blame the demon within! This is not a separate entity, but merely part of our inner selves.

This dark inner self – the shadow – if not fully incorporated, can also be projected from someone into a dark energy force that with enough emotional input can gain a life of its own. If fed with enough negative emotional energy, in the form of fear for instance, such entities can be set against others and do great harm. I would point out here that such occurrences are very rare and that in most cases these things are more imaginary, but they can happen. Those working along a path of black magic can develop ways of creating these entities and, whilst such people will eventually pay severely through the three-fold law in one way or another, they can do a lot of damage in the meantime. The key to dealing with such things is to remember that these entities can only thrive when there is negative emotion energy to feed them. If you feel the presence of such an entity and become emotionally involved with it in a negative way then it will continue to affect you or those around you. If you refuse to offer it the negative energy it demands then it will wither and fade. There is often, among witches, a temptation to fight fire with fire, especially those working along any number of delusional paths. They may get a sense of power and use this energy to frighten their foes, and once these people discover that black magic is being used against them, they fight back with similar energies. Such a situation creates a downward spiral for all concerned. You cannot fight a negative energy with more negativity, that will just offer the force what it needs to feed on and grow. You need to simply let it bounce off you and return to its sender. I would emphasise here, that it is unwise to allow any sense of paranoia to set in. Such occurrences are very rare. The average so-called witch who feels able to create such entities is usually so self-deluded that they have no real power at all – they have lessons to learn, leave them alone to learn their lessons without affecting you! It can be useful to have a small amount of protection up around you, but please don't feel that you need to undertake elaborate rituals as this would simply indicate that you are letting the fear affect you, you need to rise above such things and let the inner light of your own development reflect any darkness back to where it came from.

CONNECTING WITH TREE SPIRITS

Trees contain strong spirits that can teach us much wisdom if we are open to the lessons. Connecting with trees can be a powerful way of tapping into that wisdom. To pick a tree to work with, you could use the tree lore to find one that is associated with what you feel you need to learn, but it is often much better to use your instinct and intuition. Ensure you get plenty of opportunities to be amongst trees. Even in a big city there are usually plenty of parks available where you can sit, though the open countryside is far better. Whilst walking amongst the trees put out a mental call to the Goddess to guide you to a tree that will help you grow or bring you the energy you require. Most often you will soon feel a magnetic attraction towards a particular tree, this is the one to work with.

The easiest way to do this is to walk around the tree three times, tap on its bark three times, then talk to the tree and ask it if it is willing to work with you and help guide you. The tree does not understand English, but its spirit can pick up on a profound level the intent behind the words which need not be spoken aloud. As long as you continue to feel the magnetic attraction, then you can either sit down underneath it with your back to the trunk, or stand against it, or even embrace it. If you wish you can put a mental Circle up around both yourself and the tree to strengthen the connection. Close your eyes and visualise yourself becoming part of the tree itself. Feel the roots delving deep into the earth, the strong tall trunk with its branches reaching towards the sky and swaying in the breeze – taking nourishment from the light and air. You are one with the tree. Just open your heart and mind and see what comes to you. When you have finished, thank the spirit of the tree and leave a small gift to show your gratitude. Remember to remove the Circle if you mentally cast one.

GAINING ENERGY FROM TREES

With their roots going deep into the earth and their branches in the sky, trees are potential sources of great energy. They are more than willing to help you by sharing that energy if you are going to use it for the good of all. As before, you need to be guided to trees that are going to be the best for offering you the sort of energy you require. Using your logical functions by studying tree lore is rarely the best way to do this – you need to use your intuition.

Find two trees of the same kind that are close together. Ideally you need them within touching distance of each other. Ask the trees for their blessing. Stand between the trees and close your eyes opening your heart and mind to their energies. You will begin to feel the energy of the trees and yours become as one as long as you fully open yourself up. Gradually allow the energy to flow through you as if the two trees and yourself were as one. Once again, thank the trees when you have finished and remember to leave an offering.

11

SELF DEVELOPMENT AND THE PROCESS OF INITIATION

Spiritual development is the process of connecting the lower self as experienced during an incarnation with the Higher Self known by the soul. The physical plane is at one end of the spectrum of the planes of existence, with the spiritual at the other end. Being able to span these planes and experience the divine contact known by the soul and the comparative vulgarity of the physical at the same time is more than one lifetime's work. Such contact, when it is eventually made, comes initially in short enlightening glimpses or flashes. Steady dedicated practice and work over many years can gradually move those brief experiences from being momentary to being more prolonged, eventually becoming more and more a part of everyday life, though the work required is usually extraordinarily challenging. But then manifesting the spiritual plane on the physical (or as Christians would say – 'building heaven on earth') is hardly likely to be an easy task!

At the time of writing, as we enter the Aquarian Age, there are people incarnating at all levels of development from the most basic and primitive to those quite advanced and capable of guiding others. The energies of the Aquarian Age are asserting a quickening of this development process and all sorts of new systems are emerging to aid this process of which Wicca is just one. Every individual will be facing challenges to one degree or another, but cultures as a whole will also be facing tremendous challenges that need to be overcome such as war, poverty, hunger, etc. The war in Iraq is just one example of many deadly and damaging conflicts from which we need, as a race, to learn some serious lessons as the Aquarian energies of group harmony are to be successfully embraced.

DEVELOPMENT – STAGES ONE TO TWO

For those at the most basic and primitive stage of development there is no conscious awareness of any spiritual involvement in life. The communication from the soul is entirely unconscious and yet still effective. It is necessary for these people to live a life full of experience at an animal and emotional level; their energy will be focused on and dominated by the base chakra energy point working through the bottom of the spine and the genitals. Several incarnations at this level gradually build experience that is gathered and assimilated at the spiritual level. The experience of growth will eventually lead to contact with the soul and towards understanding that at this stage is totally missing during incarnation.

DEVELOPMENT – STAGES THREE TO FOUR

For those incarnating with more experience – what some might call the 'average' person – the life is still consciously unaware of the soul communication, though there is a niggling feeling beginning to arouse every now and then that there is an unseen driving force behind the personality. It is the work of these incarnating individuals to continue the growth experience and respond fully to the drive of the personality using the gut reactions manifesting through the solar plexus energy point. This helps to build an integrated personality that will eventually be of greater use for the soul's control.

DEVELOPMENT – STAGE FIVE

At the next level of incarnation – what we might call the 'aspirant' – the person becomes aware of the soul contact behind the personality. The person starts to experience the pull from the soul and recognising that the personality itself is not the real self. This can be a particularly unsettling experience that can cause all sorts of reactions from fanaticism and mental disorder to physical ills. It is a long and painful process, and one that will be experienced through many lives as the energies from below the diaphragm develop further and start integrating through the solar plexus to the heart centre. Steadying the energies at the heart centre energy point is eventually achieved through many painful trials and errors.

DEVELOPMENT – STAGE SIX

At the next stage the incarnating person experiences far greater stimulation and vitalisation of the energy centres, particularly those above the diaphragm. A conscious awareness of the soul is now far more prevalent though the communication is still far from clear. The whole physical body is becoming inspired by contact from the other planes through the energy centres and the person needs to learn to control and balance these energies. Regular and inevitable imbalances will occur leading to many negative experiences, but as the lessons of these experiences are learned then progress is made. It is at this stage that a person is most likely to respond well to the guidance of a High Priestess and/or High Priest and work within a group.

It is also at this stage that a spiritual guide may be putting in a great deal of effort in order to progress the incarnation towards the final stages of initiation possible on the physical plane. Rapid progress is possible, though the failures can produce even greater crashes (more likely at a mental as such a person will be working primarily on a mental plane level).

There will be many cases from this level that get stuck at a deep emotional level which will be displayed as one of the self-deluding glamours. At each stage of development it is easy to conclude, due to the vast opening of energies previously not experienced, that the person has reached the pinnacle of development; this is the seed that develops into delusion. Having struggled through some very difficult stages and experiences it can become quite humbling and sometimes even disconcerting to realise that there is still more to come. The path does not get easier, in fact it gets even rockier with even deeper pitfalls, we just gain the strength to face what is ahead of us or submit to the realisation that we have done as much as we have planned for one lifetime.

At this stage the person is most likely to increasingly appreciate that the path that has meant so much to them, and helped them pull all the pieces of the jigsaw together, is only one of many valid paths. The one that has been followed – possibly a Celtic-inspired Wiccan path – may have proven to be the path most suited to this individual. An esoteric Christian path may well suit the next person much better. Neither path is right or wrong, though only one is likely to be right for each individual, the paths are just different. They are suited to a different kind of mind, a different cultural up-bringing, different interpretations of the symbols. The end result of any path is the same, even though it may be interpreted in a multitude of ways.

DEVELOPMENT – STAGE SEVEN AND BEYOND

The last stage within the incarnation process is to have achieved a balance between each energy centre within the etheric body. The whole physical vehicle will be open and responsive to the soul and the ray energy it is working through. Each energy centre will be finely tuned to that ray energy and will have confined the other ray energies to being in their proper place, subsidiary to that ray. In Wicca this is achievable beyond the third degree of initiation. The third degree, if properly taken when ready, is not the end in itself, but is the beginning of the end. A third degree should be working primarily on the spiritual and mental planes. Such a person is perfectly capable of working on any of the planes with control, though there will be few times when it is deemed appropriate to work on the emotional levels. The person is now working for the needs of the group and has an unselfish outlook; the person could be decentralised in it regarding its own personal life. Once fully achieved this stage will enable the initiate to break free of disease within the physical body. The focus of attention is through the higher mental planes towards the soul and the group of souls with which it is most closely associated.

Upon death it is likely that further incarnation is not required for development beyond this last stage, though this may be chosen in order to help others or further the work of the divine from the physical plane. If choosing not to incarnate, then the initiate will have other choices through which to serve, including becoming a spiritual guide to help others.

Those attracted to Wicca, and other pagan or ritualistic paths, are most likely to be responding both to the sense of change created by the in-coming Age of Aquarius as well as the specific ray energy that Age works through – the seventh ray of Ceremonial Magic and Order. Those attracted to Wicca (with the exception of those who think it is simply about casting love spells and working magic to enhance oneself) will almost certainly have developed to the stage of an aspirant and will be looking for a system that offers answers to the many questions forming in their minds. These questions are planted there by the soul as a way of guiding the physical vehicle back in its direction in the hope that the answers found on the physical will continue to open up the body to the full range of reality. Once soul contact is achieved and communication has consciously opened to the degree where that communication is reasonably clear, then experience on the physical plane can be fed directly to the spiritual and increase the rate of growth considerably.

WICCAN THREE DEGREE SYSTEM

One of the things that defines Wicca as a system is the process of the three degrees of initiation. This is how it was developed by its founders. It was never intended to be a path for a solo witch, even though certain authors have borrowed the name of Wicca in such a context. (Wicca was first presented as a solitary path in the USA by Scott Cunningham, probably in an effort to cut through the heavy negative connotations associated with the word 'witch' in a country where prejudice still runs at a high level.)

The way a Wiccan group works most effectively on the process of spiritual growth is by having access to a well-developed High Priestess/High Priest who has properly attained the third degree. In an ideal scenario it is preferable for the group to be led by a High Priestess with an equally developed High Priest as her consort, though this luxury is not always readily possible. The elders within the group act as guides and tutors and apply all that is required to help those others within the group to develop at an appropriate pace. A well-established group would consist of a number of people at different stages of development (at first, second and third degree) as well as an outer court of aspirants (or 'cowans') who have yet to choose to take the big first step of formal initiation.

At no point should any member of the group feel pressured in any way to progress from one degree to the next. It is not necessarily the case that each member will achieve third degree in this incarnation. The High Priestess and/or High Priest must use her/his judgement wisely. It would be a crime to hold anyone back from initiation who is clearly ready to progress, but it would be an even worse crime to force through initiates who are not ready in an effort bolster the group. Any High Priestess/High Priest who forces people through when they are ill-prepared takes on a great deal of responsibility and will inevitably answer to the Threefold Law of Return. There are, unfortunately, many who think they have attained third degree who simply haven't. This lack of quality control (only to be expected in a non-hierarchical system) will reflect on those they teach and will eventually result in the group falling apart, though not without some considerable heart-ache. Even in such a situation, however, there are many valuable lessons to be learned, though some will obviously sadly conclude that Wicca isn't the path for them and chuck the baby out with the bath water.

Whether the student is a Wiccan in a group, or working solo, there is always plenty of inner personal work to be conducted during meditations. A Wiccan isn't dependent in any way to a particular group – the group could be organised in many different ways, often quite loosely.

THE 'SECRET OF TRANSLATION'

Spiritual aspiration is not an emotional attitude, but the driving force towards enlightenment and the realisation of Oneness with the Goddess and God and the whole of creation, including every other soul. To borrow a theosophical term, the elevating power of the aspiration is the key to the 'Secret of Translation'. The Secret of Translation is expressed when aspiration is allowed free rein which, when followed with the sincerity of motive and pure love, brings about three things:

(1) The stimulation of the higher sub-planes within each of the seven planes.
(2) A lessening of the effect of the lower sub-planes due to this higher stimulation which further loosens the bond to the physical plane.
(3) The 'magnetic attraction' of other atoms that are already working at a higher vibration towards those of your own. This may bring about an increase in what be termed 'occult phenomena' to be experienced. The further this process continues, the more readily accepted are these phenomena.

It should be noted here that 'atoms of a higher vibration' are drawn to the person through a process best described as 'magnetic attraction' rather than the force of will as is commonly thought. The will of the soul works on the atoms already present within the body and can raise that body's vibrations which automatically attracts those higher vibrating atoms from outside the body. All of our bodies are made from atoms that have been recycling themselves in various forms on the physical plane throughout the ages – this is not a metaphysical theory but a scientifically accepted fact. Energy cannot be destroyed, only transformed. The atoms vibrating on a higher level are, to a certain degree, things that have yet to be fully understood by modern 'orthodox' science, but have been understood by occultists throughout the ages (though through the work of quantum physics the orthodox scientists are beginning to catch up at last).

Within Wicca there are many disciplines available that help create this magnetically attractive situation. The useful mix of these disciplines will depend to a large degree on the type of person pursuing them. A High Priestess or High Priest should be able to offer the candidate appropriate guidance. It can be of enormous help to have someone to turn to that is not only experienced, but also capable of being objective. This is one of the advantages of working as part of a Wiccan group or coven rather than as a solitary where few opportunities for such guidance exist (presuming, of course, that the group has a teacher who has properly achieved third degree status).

The 'occult phenomena' mentioned above could include things such as hearing noises (or voices); raised intuitive skills; sensitivity to energies of all kinds; an increase in synchronistic occurrences; etc. Someone who already has any of these skills may have a natural talent (though they may be on the way to developing schizophrenia) but this would not automatically suggest that the whole person has reached this stage of development.

When a Wiccan takes the first degree initiation she or he aspires for union with the Goddess and God. This is only an aspiration; the initiate is neither entirely bound, nor entirely free to turn away though turning away is still an option. The first degree Wiccan should have reached the point where she or he is reasonably certain that Wicca is the path intended for them. The role is not particularly challenging at this stage. They will be expected to learn to cast circles, to be able to make the appropriate invocations, and to show appropriate respect to the spirits of the other planes including the elementals. (Learning to cast circles is more than simply learning an appropriate forms of words, but includes learning how to open oneself up enough to channel the energies from the other planes.)

The situation is different once the initiate has taken the second degree. She or he has made the decision to become bound to the path; there is no turning back (and there will be times they wish they could!). This is a matter that needs thorough consideration before taking the second degree. Once the second degree has been taken, the initiate no longer aspires for union, but has chosen to train for that union. At some point along the path from second degree to third the applicant must prove the lower and Higher Self ready for such union and undergo a regime of strict discipline. This discipline is optional only once the union at third degree has been successfully achieved though many will appreciate the wisdom of incorporating it into the daily life, though even then the path is not an easy one and requires reality constant checks.

It has been known in Wicca, all too often, for far too little time and attention to be spent on initiates at the second degree level. It has even been known for the second and third degrees to be taken together. This is something that should be discouraged as the development process between these levels is highly challenging and often unavoidably traumatic. Rushing through this process would only create High Priestesses and High Priests suffering the glamour of ego inflation, resulting in covens of poor quality and individuals whose contribution to the work of the Goddess and God is effectively nil (though the self-deluded will be convinced that they have developed an indispensable relationship with the divine).

At second degree the initiate is usually given the title of High Priestess or High Priest for the first time. They are given the opportunity to personify the Goddess or God within a cast Circle. By personifying these archetypes one is potentially introducing some highly powerful energies (it is far more than an elaborate role-playing game, in fact not a game at all). Both the title and the role creates a situation where that person's ego can easily become highly inflated. However, the intension is for the teacher to guide that person to overcome this natural reaction before it becomes both self destructive and a disruptive influence within the coven. If the teacher has not developed the skills to successfully guide that person through the process, maybe because they have never made it through themselves, then (at best) there is the risk of destroying the group and creating initiates with severe cases of self-delusion.

All of this should highlight the importance of ensuring you find a good teacher if you are entering the initiation process. If you are a teacher, or training to be one, it should emphasise the responsibility of your undertaking and importance of constantly questioning yourself as to your proper development. (If when asking yourself whether or not you are up to the challenge your immediate reaction is to doubt, and then after thorough consideration you conclude that you are, then this is a positive indication. If you never doubt that you are up to the challenge, then chances are that you are deluding yourself and those under your wing.)

All this may sound quite negative and daunting. It should certainly offer an explanation as to why Wicca could not possibly be correctly described as a path for the solitary. However, it should be pointed out that there are some very good teachers, you just need to be cautious rather than to allow your enthusiasm to overcome discretion.

The following notes and commentaries offer guidance on the level of discipline and attitudes within the lower mind that are expected before the third degree initiation can be successfully undertaken. The words in italics have been inspired by, and paraphrase, the work of theosophists, theosophy being one of the many inspirations of modern day Wicca:

Note 1 – The initiate must honestly and objectively consider the motives within the heart. If there is truly an unconditional love for all her or his brothers and sisters, and little concern for herself or himself, this is a sign that the initiate is becoming ready for the third degree initiation. Each of us has gone through many incarnations in order to gain numerous experiences that are gathered by our Higher Selves. Once our understanding of this process reaches a reasonably advanced level we begin to fully appreciate that we are serving a far greater purpose than that originally imagined by our lower self and that we are but a tiny part of a greater whole, though many will suffer delusions of grandeur on the way to this realisation. We also reach the point where we understand that all our brothers and sisters on the physical plane are also going through this same process and that the same spirit that drives them works through us too; we are literally brothers and sisters and thus part of a vast family. Part of our task is to help our brothers and sisters to experience all that they can in order to progress towards conscious reunion with the Goddess and God, especially those within our own soul group. By understanding that we are already immortal we realise that there is no need to be overly concerned about our fate in life, though we should treat it with the deepest of respect and not waste it. Whatever happens to us will be of value to our souls whether we experience it as pleasant or otherwise.

Note 2 – If the initiate asks for the third degree initiation physically, emotionally and mentally, then the time is not yet right. There are a great many people who have been taken through a third degree ritual who quite clearly have not fully advanced to that stage of development. The glamour of being a third degree High Priestess or High Priest is a compelling one for those suffering from illusions of grandeur on the physical, emotional and/or mental planes. To serve the Goddess and God we need to be humble, knowing that we are but a tiny cog in a very big machine. We need to appreciate the seriousness of the role we are to perform. We need to be willing to serve the Goddess and God for their own sakes and not our own with all the sacrifice it entails. Until the illusions on the physical, emotional and mental levels within the individual have broken down and the initiate is ready to serve in any way the gods choose to use us, from a spiritual perspective, then we are not truly ready for the third degree initiation and any ritual undertaken will be meaningless and cause problems for others.

Note 3 – The call towards union with the Goddess and God is triple in nature and this call will be heard by the higher guides and spirits resulting in the removal of the veil that hides the door. When the initiate is ready to serve as a third degree she or he will have been working towards that service on the physical, emotional and mental levels for some time. On the physical level the initiate will blossom like a rose and appear at perfect ease with the physical self. On the emotional level the 'restless waters' will have become stilled and will not be the guiding factor for the lower self. On the mental level, clarity will have been maintained that enables the initiate to see her or his humble role in the great scheme. Once the initiate has attuned her or himself to the energies coming from the soul on all three of these levels and the life is working in harmony, then the next initiation will occur whether a physical ritual is undertaken or not; nothing can prevent it. It is not the ritual itself that turns a second degree Wiccan into a third degree, but the opening of the veil. The ritual simply helps the initiate to move through the already open door. The ritual can help bring open those energies through its symbolic form, but if the initiate is not truly ready then the veil will remain just another illusion. If the veil isn't truly removed and the door opened, no ritual will force it open.

Note 4 – The initiate will need to tend the spiritual fires of evolution to help nourish the physical lives of the brothers and sisters in order to keep the wheels turning. Becoming a third degree High Priestess or High Priest is not about removing oneself from the responsibilities one has on the physical plane, quite the reverse, it creates greater responsibilities. It is important to continue to keep oneself grounded in the physical, to continue to keep one's physical affairs in order, and to continue to work at the relationships with those around us. Our task is to bring the planes together as one reality, not to retreat to the mental and spiritual realms as we do in between incarnations. It is, therefore, just as important to recognise the importance of the physical plane and to show respect for it as it is for the spiritual. By working as a third degree we will be looked upon for inspiration and as an example. If we manage to inspire and set a good example then we will be helping to keep the spiritual flame in those around us nourished for growth as well as ensuring we show respect for the physical manifestations of the Goddess and God that we experience in nature.

Note 5 – The initiate will learn to stand in the light and dim the fires of the lower self. A third degree High Priestess or High Priest needs to maintain the connection with the spiritual plane, though for the first few years of going through the initiation there will be times when this connection is temporarily lost. All initiates go through a period of adjustment where the difficult role and weight of responsibility is learnt to be carried with ease. At third degree the initiate has raised her or his spirit to its proper place – above the other four elements (having mastered them), and above the emotional plane where the lower ego resides. The initiate will still be in touch and recognise (clearly) the ego of the lower self, both its personality and its shadow, but will no longer be ruled by it.

Note 6 – The physical body must be nourished with energy and refrain from taking the life of another in order ensure the etheric body functions without hindrance. The quality of the physical body needs to be maintained in good order. There should no longer be any need for taking physical nourishment into the body via the flesh of lesser souls as the initiate's karma should have reached the point of equilibrium. Energy needs to flow unhindered into the physical body, through its etheric element, from all levels so that the spiritual, mental and emotional energy is clearly visible to all who care to look.

Note 7 – The sound must ring forth on the spiritual plane in a pure voice in order to attract the attentions of our guides and assure them that we are ready to step forward. Having undertaken the work at the first and second degree levels with the necessary discipline, then the raised vibrations (the sound) on the upper mental plane attract the attention of those higher spiritual guides who will (metaphorically) take us by the hand and guide us through the final stages of growth. They know when you are ready, will recognise you and know the work you have put in. If you are not ready they will most likely throw obstacles in your way that will need to be taken as lessons from which we learn what we have missed until we have truly cleared the way. There is no way to fool these spirits, and any amount of pleading will only serve to confirm to them that we haven't yet achieved the necessary vibration.

Note 8 – When the second degree initiate nears the third degree veil, the Greater Seven must awaken and bring forth a response from the lesser seven upon the double circle. The 'Greater Seven' in this context refers to the universal energies that flow through the seven planes, sometimes referred to as 'the seven rays'. The 'lesser seven upon the double circle' refers to those energies as they relate to us as individual incarnations in both their positive and negative aspects – this is represented by the vesica pisces that is described in the chapter on symbols and shown in another form in Figure 54. As the initiate approaches third degree the energies working through the seven major energy centres (the etheric interface) that link the physical body with the other planes become stronger. The communication, for want of a more accurate term, that comes to us through (not exactly 'from') the planets in the form of the seven rays becomes clearer and has an effect on the physical body that can, at first, be quite unsettling. The physical organs and glands throughout the body

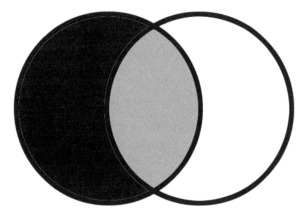

▲ *Figure 54 – The double Circle representing the Goddess and God within, with all the positive and negative, passive and receptive elements with which we need to find a balance*

experience a change that requires patience and understanding on the part of the initiate and the teacher. Once the physical body accepts the changes and the development process is in a more advanced condition, the sense of disruption settles down gently into its new rhythm. To force this development through experimentation can bring disastrous results such as deep depression, anxiety and stress resulting in any manner of physical ills. A good teacher must learn to recognise when this stage has been reached. An initiate who wants an relatively easy ride (and the 'ease' is only relative) will tend to refrain from forcing development of any of the individual centres and restrict themselves to a theoretical study of the energy centres and the meaning of service to the Goddess and God. It is through the comprehension that this study brings about that enables a patient and relatively smooth transition through this difficult transition. The rate of development is controlled on levels beyond the physical and emotional to ensure a transition that is thorough and suited to the candidate, each of whom will experience it in different ways. The gods, your guides and your Higher Self know what they are doing; it is best to allow them to get on with their job and remain receptive by comprehending the general process and purpose. There may be times when the energies seem to be growing in intensity at an alarming rate, and others when no development is occurring. This is quite normal. The energies tend to stop growing in intensity to allow time for the physical body to assimilate the changes. The temptation to speed the process is quite natural but guaranteed to fail. This would be a sign of impatience and also that there may be glamours (egotistical illusions within the lower self) that still need to be addressed. Throughout this period the initiate will benefit from keeping a careful and thorough record of the changes experienced through this transitional process. This record is for the benefit of the initiate and, in order to gain further guidance and encouragement, should be open for the teacher to survey and comment on in a sensitive manner and thus further aid the process. The journal can form part of the initiate's Book of Shadows and will be of great value when the time comes for taking others through the same process, though many will choose to keep such notes separate. Having an experienced and trustworthy teacher (and there is no other kind worthy of the title 'teacher') is a great benefit if not an absolute necessity in this regard, though the teaching function can be entirely undertaken by a spiritual guide in some rare cases. This sort of development is extremely difficult for those on a solitary path and therefore one of the reasons Wicca (as a group activity) has a great advantage in the growth process.

Note 9 – The initiate needs to merge and blend with the totality of the soul's experience. Through this exercise one can find those who belong to one's own group and begin to work together openly to further the divine plan. Having fully appreciated the process of birth, death and rebirth, the initiate can then obtain an understanding that opens channels to the whole of the soul's experiences gained through past lives. This usually comes in small doses as to suddenly have the full range of experiences opened up would create a shock and an overload that few could deal with adequately. Having reached this level there will be an enormous range of experiences to accept and some of them will inevitably appear quite unpleasant. Once again, patience is a strong ally in this stage of development. Learn to go with the flow and deal with the issues the memories dredge up one by one. Those who are ready to progress significantly will find that there are some memories that appear quite disturbing at first. It is when we step back in order to appreciate the lessons learned that we are able to console ourselves that even the most negative experiences have positive outcomes. A sense of guilt for past-life failures is pointless and must be avoided; we cannot change the past, only learn from it and grow in order to use those negative experiences for positive gain. If we do not experience the dark how can we ever fully appreciate the light? How can we experience positive if there is no negative? It is all a matter of balance – and part of the balance Wiccans seek by working with the Goddess and God in all Their aspects.

Note 10 – The initiate must learn how to master the elements in all their forms and learn how to apply their functions in an appropriate manner. The elements of Earth, Air, Fire and Water are each directed by elementals, spirits that have not chosen the path of reincarnation, but which have chosen to undertake a different and important role. It is important to differentiate between the elements and the elementals; one aims to learn intelligent control of the elements, but respect the elementals. The spirits of the elements may appear to us in the form of fairies, undines, salamanders, gnomes or any other guises. In reality they have no such form that we would recognise from our range of physical experiences. They will, during the stage where we are still ruled by our lower ego, tend to create situations for us that make us feel uncomfortable. This is not from a stance of trickery or malice (though it may well seem like it); we can learn and grow by working through these situations, or help those around us learn and grow from our experience of them. Eventually we need to learn to master the elements. The attitude that we should be seeking is not a mastery that demands respect, but the mastery as that of a concert musician over her or his instrument – one of great respect.

Note 11 – The energies that have developed within the lower three centres need to be mirrored in those of the upper three whilst maintaining the lower through the heart centre. The energy centres below the diaphragm (root, sacral and solar plexus) are the ones that develop most readily and bring the energy that drives our physical body and our emotions. These energies need to begin to rise up through the body, be mirrored in the upper three energy centres, and work through all seven energy centres in harmony. This is another example of the maxim 'as above, so below' and the hexagram symbol, with a point in the centre representing the heart, can readily represent this. Just as with cylinders in an engine, if each one is working efficiently, working at a similar level without too much restriction, then they work together in harmony. The heart centre is the central pivotal point through which these energies begin to flow together once harmony is approached. Eventually the energy will, if successful, flow through the root chakra and crown chakra as one without any restriction.

Note 12 – The initiate will learn to use the hands, feet and eye in a way that serves the Goddess and God. The things we do on the physical plane need to be in harmony with the service we are offering the Goddess and God. The 'eye' in this respect refers to the third eye, the energy centre through which we see beyond the physical. This, therefore, implies that the service that we apply ourselves to is not limited to the physical plane, but to all the planes and a potentially vast array of work that could come to us (often unexpectedly) from any level.

A NOTE ON RELATIONSHIPS

The process of spiritual development, at least in its early stages, is a very personal affair. Those who do aspire to grow and develop will inevitably find themselves in a relationship that can cause all sorts of problems. Each partner will inevitably have a differing world-view. The extent of this difference will vary. If one partner is a Pagan and the other a Christian, this need not cause too many problems if each respects the other's views and neither is particularly active or dogmatic in their worship. The passive state is perfectly normal in every form of spirituality. However, spiritual development cannot be entirely passive – that would be the way of the mystic. Development comes through actively participating with the energies from the other planes through an esoteric tradition and is occult, rather than mystic, in nature. It is when these energies come into play and the development brings the inevitable changes to oneself that problems can come into play. If your partner remains entirely passive to his or her own development, then the revelations that you receive may well seem strange ('whacky') to your partner. There may come a time when you both feel that you are growing apart, and this may be the case.

To avoid a split you will need to find a balance between explaining to your partner what you are doing and experiencing, whilst protecting him or her from information that will cause a conflict in their mental understanding that is beyond comprehension. Unless one is experiencing the development, and seeing beyond the illusions of the physical and emotional planes, then there are some things that are, by default, simply beyond comprehension. It is possible that, to avoid a split, then you may need to take some time out from your development programme in order for the situation to settle. You may, of course, develop so far beyond the emotional level that you realise that to go your separate ways, without any hard feelings, is best for both of you. This would most often be the case in a relationship that was initially based on an emotional co-dependence. Emotional dependence is a form of mutual energy vampirism that will become painful as your higher functions develop. It would be like undermining your foundations!

None of this will be much of a problem if two partners are developing together and at relatively similar rates. Bear in mind, however, that the relationships we go through are most often part of the necessary karmic activity, the variety of life experiences, that we need in order to grow as a Soul. Good and 'bad' experiences are needed to gain enlightenment and reach the point of ascension.

If you are working occultly with your partner, then you will find this very difficult if your levels of development are different. Some say that you should never work with someone on a different level. I maintain that it is merely very difficult, and not impossible, and needs a great deal of consideration (particularly from the partner on the higher level). Bear in mind that you will be communicating in different ways both consciously and unconsciously. Someone whose stage of development dictates that the main focus of their energy is on the emotional plane (at first, and possibly second, degree for instance) will not communicate well with someone whose focus is on the mental and spiritual planes without practice, due consideration and understanding.

BUILDING THE RAINBOW BRIDGE

The Rainbow Bridge is known in Buddhist philosophy as the 'Antah-karana'. It is the bridge built between the lower self and the soul and is a process that was actually begun (hopefully) at the time of approaching the first degree, even if it wasn't realised at the time. As a third degree Wiccan it is your job to straddle this Bridge so that the energies of the spiritual plane and the physical plane work as smoothly as if they were one and the same. This is not as easy as it sounds. Having reached third degree it should occur to you that this is where the hard lessons really begin to form ... and you thought it had been hard up to this point? Think again! Very few third degree Wiccans successfully manage to build the Rainbow Bridge (although in effect this is what is being done during the third degree initiation). Even fewer manage to straddle the Bridge and maintain the difficult balancing act required to stand there. It can come with practice – but expect some serious bruising on both the physical, emotional and mental planes during this process which can take many years of sincere effort and practice.

The strands that make up the Rainbow Bridge are the Seven Rays and all the energies that they bring. Whilst the foundations of this Bridge are inevitably laid throughout the initiation process, it would be folly for this work to continue on a conscious level while dealing with the many issues surrounding illusion and glamour at the lower degrees. It is difficult for anyone dealing with issues of illusion (as real and as solid as these illusions appear at the time) to appreciate that the higher initiations (beyond third degree) are free from all physical, emotional and mental concern. It is hard for a cowan or an initiate to even contemplate the idea that the whole experience of emotion, for example, is a complete illusion that

▲ *Figure 55 – The Hexagram – the foundation of the Rainbow Bridge*

has little or no significance. Many would actually find such a statement quite alien and cold, maybe even repugnant, as they value these emotional illusions so highly (which is why it is so hard to let go of them). The initiate needs to have risen above the self-centred reactions to the work, risen above the need to satisfy the lower egotistical self, as the work from here deals directly with our goddesses and gods on the spiritual plane. Even the 'spiritual urge' itself needs to be let go of, as this itself is a self-centred attitude. You just need to 'be'. It is at this point that the Master guide on the ray on which you work will fully recognise that it is time to take you by the hand and guide you forwards to play a full part in fulfilling the divine plan. You will need to set aside all your personal aspirations and be open to the aspirations of these higher entities, ready to serve them as they demand, whatever the task, however small your lower-self may feel that task really is.

At the first degree initiation we are given the symbol of the downward pointing triangle, representing the completion of the lower triad of functions of the personality. At the third initiation we are given the upward pointing triangle, representing the higher spiritual triad, the union with the Goddess, God and divine source. The structure of the Rainbow Bridge is based on the combination of these two triangles, forming a hexagram (Figure 55). The structural soundness of the Bridge is dependent on the structural soundness of those completed triads. If there is a weakness within either triad then the Bridge will be weak, too weak to cross and you certainly will not get to the point where you can attempt that first tentative straddle. Having spent many years reaching this point it is most difficult to realise that there is in fact a weakness as it sometimes requires going back to basics in order to address those issues and to strengthen the triad. Nevertheless, if a weakness is recognised it needs to be dealt with, no matter how disheartening the process may appear – it's all part of the testing process and all part of proving your sincerity and resolve. To attempt to cross the Bridge when it has such a weakness will only result in a crashing fall that is much more painful than addressing a problem you have already recognised, but this does guarantee that we will not cross the Bridge until it is strong enough to hold our weight (or more accurately our lack of weight or burden).

The conscious building of the Rainbow Bridge can be started once the initiate is fully working on the upper mental plane with a focus of activity towards the spiritual. It is important to understand the subtle distinctions between the thinker, the process of thought, and the thought itself. Once this has been achieved one can then work on distinguishing the difference between a thought that emanates from the lower-self and one that comes from the spiritual dimension. It is necessary to distinguish between the life thread (the silver cord that directs the spirit that animates our physical being) from the consciousness thread. The life thread works primarily through the heart centre, and from there works through our entire body. The consciousness thread works through our third eye centre in our heads. This recognition will allow the initiate to become receptive to the ideas coming from the spiritual dimension and filter out those that are interfering from the lower animal self. Having achieved this, then one can then proceed to develop fully the ability to be creative on the mental plane and consciously build thought-forms that have real value.

EXERCISE – MEDITATING WITH THE HERMIT

The Hermit card in the Tarot represents the spiritual guide who lights the way towards wisdom. Take this card out of the pack and visualise yourself as the Hermit holding the lantern in front of you to guide the way. Inside the lantern, the bright light hides an image of the hexagram. Focus your attention on the light and step forward without fear towards the light and just keep walking!

This work is inevitably developed through meditation. A period of retreat may well benefit an initiate working at this level in order to find the space required for this somewhat intense work. Once the mental apparatus is fully aligned the intensity of the work can be relaxed as the required focus becomes easier to maintain and control. A 'mystic' might suggest that all you need to do to achieve enlightenment is to lead a good, spiritually sound life. This is not so. Sitting back and waiting for something to happen is inadequate, though it is indeed necessary to live as decently as you can. Being passive is not enough. The construction of the Rainbow Bridge requires an active involvement, it is brought about by a definitely directed life-tendency to always move towards enlightenment boldly and without fear, recognising, accepting and correcting the mistakes we will inevitably make along the way.

12

THE WICCAN CIRCLE

The Wiccan Circle is the usual place in which full ritual work is undertaken, whether working alone or in a group. The Circle helps to contain the power and focus the magical energy raised during ritual. A properly cast circle creates a sacred space that bridges the gap 'between the worlds' where magic can be worked on all levels. Stepping into a Circle that is properly prepared is to step into a space that spans the dimensions – a multidimensional reality broader than we generally perceive. Some people refer to it as a 'circle of protection', which can be quite misleading. Before casting your Circle it is necessary to cleanse the area of any residue energies that are present and then put up a barrier around that area to enclose it. This does, in effect, 'protect' those within the Circle from outside influences that may interfere with the purity of your work, but it should not be thought that there is anything outside the Circle to be feared. You are basically carving out a sacred space that brings the physical, emotional, mental and spiritual planes closer together, ideally as one, and therefore it is necessary to create that barrier between your sacred space and the mundane plane outside.

In my first book, *Wiccan Spirituality*, I detailed the standard basic Circle casting procedure. There are a few points from that book that are worth repeating before I describe a more advanced form of Circle casting.

First of all, the size of the Circle is important. Wiccan tradition has come to suggest that the ideal Circle should be nine feet in diameter, and to measure this one uses your nine-foot (three times three yard) cords to mark out the space. A nine-foot Circle is, in my opinion, far too small in most circumstances – certainly too small for a small group of witches, let alone a full thirteen member coven! The Circle is not actually a flat circle but a *sphere* of power. Even though its centre is cast from the level of your heart chakra (rather than from a point on the floor) nine feet barely gives a single person room to move without breaking the circumference which is best avoided (though not drastic as it tends to retain a certain elasticity). I find twelve feet much more suitable for working alone or with two or three others; for larger groups I would move up to more like eighteen feet. The symbolism of the number three, sacred to the Goddess, is retained by working in twelve or eighteen feet as the numbers can be reduced numerologically to three or nine ($1 + 2 = 3$ or $1 + 8 = 9$).

Secondly, it is important to build the right atmosphere when casting a Circle and to maintain certain rules that are there for good reason. Wicca does not have many rules generally, in fact that is one of its many attractions, but there are some worth adhering to. A rule I would suggest one maintains religiously is that one *invokes* the elementals and *invites* the Goddess and God (or any specific goddesses and/or gods you may be working with). Only a black magician would be so arrogant as to *demand* the participation of a goddess or god by *invoking* them, but it is fine to *invoke* the elementals as by the time you are working as a High Priestess or High Priest your spirit should have attained the level of mastering the elements. I use the word *master* in the context of a musician *mastering* her or his instrument rather than as a master and slave. It is a mastering that retains respect.

Finally I would point out that as we are casting a sphere, I tend to bring in through visualisation not only the elements but the Goddess and God aspects from above and below. As I suggested above, the Circle is cast from the level of the heart centre. The energies below that centre are raised up through your feet and the energies above that centre are brought down through your crown. I see these twin forces as those of black and white, light and dark, Goddess and God – the balance we work with in Wicca. The final Circle or *Sphere of Power* could therefore be depicted as in Figure 56.

THE CELESTIAL CIRCLE CASTING TECHNIQUE

In my first book, *Wiccan Spirituality*, I detailed the standard Circle casting technique that many will be familiar with. Here I am going to offer a more advanced technique that has been handed down to me called the *Celestial Circle* technique. In many ways this is actually simpler, but it is offered for those with more experience as the basic technique using an altar and the four quarters placed in the four directions contains a lot of useful symbolism that is required less for those who have had plenty of experience. The items on the altar are only symbols, they

▲ *Figure 56 – The Circle or 'Sphere of Power' uses the heart centre as its central point*

have no power in themselves other than that which comes through the participants through that symbolism. With experience comes the ability to have no great need for such symbolism, though Wiccans can obviously choose what to use when according to their own needs and circumstances. If working with others with little experience it may be best to stick to what they are familiar with, otherwise there will most likely be some unwelcome distractions.

The *Celestial Circle* technique uses the pentagram to draw down the energies in order from the spiritual plane to the physical plane within the Circle, picking up the elementals in turn. The points of the pentagram, starting from its uppermost point and working as it is drawn in a clockwise direction, represent the five elements from the least 'dense' (spirit) gradually getting more dense (through fire, air, water) to the most dense (earth) as in Figure 57. Note here that when facing spirit the active masculine (God) elements are on the right hand side and the passive feminine (Goddess) elements are on the left, just as they would be on an altar.

▲ *Figure 57 – The elements on the pentagram*

In this casting, after normal preparation such as cleansing the area and preparing the participants, an initial outer perimeter is cast using your fingers or an athame. After that, the Goddess and God (or specific goddesses and gods as appropriate) are invited from the northern-most point of the pentacle; then the elementals are invoked in turn from their respective positions using the appropriate pentagram invocation. The casting is completed by casting a second circle just inside the original perimeter either with fingers, the athame or salted water and burning incense (as symbols of the elements). Candles can be used to mark the points on the pentagram, coloured if you so choose, but are not entirely necessary. Items representing the elements can be placed in front of their respective points, especially if these are going to be used during the ritual, but there is no specific need for them in the casting. An altar can be placed in the north if desired and/or useful for storing items required, but the Circle can be cast without any tools whatsoever if desired and will successfully create a sacred space between the planes as long as the High Priestess and/or High Priest is experienced enough.

I prefer to undertake such castings skyclad when there is nobody present likely to be offended by my nakedness. Once you become used to working in this way the energies flow much more naturally and if you work in a group, as long as the group is as loving and trusting as it should be, greater results can be obtained. However, those new to working may feel shy about being naked (and no pressure should ever be put on them to remove their clothes). Working outside also helps energies to flow much more smoothly and is highly recommended, but working outside skyclad, in the British climate at least, can only be done comfortably on rare occasions without getting cold. Being comfortable is a prime consideration.

CASTING THE CELESTIAL CIRCLE

The following ritual is written for High Priestess and High Priest, but it can be done alone. If in a group then the High Priestess would normally devolve responsibility for various parts or not as she so chooses. In this version I have used candles to mark the five elements, and this is recommended, but not entirely necessary if you are able to feel the area well.

The space is cleared and cleansed in the normal way and swept from the centre outwards in a widdershins direction to remove any energies. The participants are bathed and prepared as appropriate.

Place your first candle in the north. This would best be either white or purple. Next place the other candles (either all white or red, blue, yellow and green) in order in pentagram formation (see Figure 57). If you are using any items during the ritual they can be placed in front of the candles. This leaves the centre of the Circle clear for your work. An altar can be placed in front of the north candle (north being the direction of the gods) if required. This ritual is written with an altar used, but it isn't absolutely necessary. If not using one, then any items required can be placed on the ground (the belly of the Goddess).

The High Priest makes a final check that everything required (water, wine, cakes, incense, etc.) is within the Circle.

The High Priestess then enters the Circle and stands facing the north. The High Priest follows the High Priestess and stands to her right. (Other participants would follow and stand in the centre of the Circle back to back facing outwards, evenly spaced.)

The High Priestess takes her athame and casts the initial Circle of power around the perimeter from north working deosil saying: '*This is the perimeter of our Circle . . . only love and peace may enter or leave.*'

The High Priestess returns to her original position and picks up a taper. The High Priest lights this with a match. They both move to stand in front of the northern candle.

The High Priestess says: '*Lady and Lord, Goddess and God, we stand within this, your Circle, to greet you and to do your bidding. We invite you and the assembled spirits of our Craft to enter this sacred Sphere of Power to work with us and through us for the good of all, so it must be!*'

They both bow gently. The High Priestess lights the northern candle that marks the entry point of the Goddess and God. All

▲ *Figure 58 – Invoking pentagram of Fire*

▲ *Figure 59 – Invoking pentagram of Air*

participants visualise the energies entering the Circle. The High Priest then raises his athame (in salute) and draws a line from the north candle to the fire candle. (Fire is the active masculine element.) The High Priestess follows and stands to his left in front of the candle.

The High Priest says: 'Guardians of the element of Fire, we summon, stir and call you to attend this rite and guard our Circle with the power and energy of your deepest passion.'

He then draws an invoking pentagram of Fire (Figure 58) in front of the candle, visualising and feeling the Fire elementals arriving whilst the High Priestess lights the candle with the taper. The High Priest raises his athame in salute again and continues to draw the line to the air candle. (Air is the passive masculine element.) The High Priestess follows and stands to his left in front of the candle.

The High Priest says: '*Guardians of the element of Air, we summon, stir and call you to attend this rite and guard our Circle with the power and energy of the swift winged messenger of the gods.*'

He then draws an invoking pentacle of Air (Figure 59) in front of the candle, visualising and feeling the Air elementals arriving whilst the High Priestess lights the candle with the taper. The High Priest raises his athame in salute again. The High Priestess hands the taper to the High Priest. The High Priestess now continues drawing the line to the water candle. (Water is the active feminine element.) The High Priest follows and stands to her right in front of the candle.

The High Priestess says: '*Guardians of the element of Water, we summon stir and call you to attend this rite and guard our Circle with the power and energy of the water of time and forgetfulness.*'

She then draws an invoking pentagram of Water (Figure 60) in front of the candle, visualising and feeling the Water elementals arriving whilst

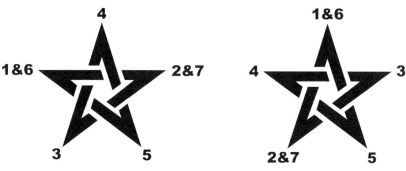

▲ *Figure 60 – Invoking pentagram of Water*

▲ *Figure 61 – Invoking pentagram of Earth*

the High Priest lights the candle with the taper. The High Priestess raises her athame in salute again. The High Priestess now continues drawing the line to the earth candle. (Earth is the passive feminine element.) The High Priest follows and stands to her right in front of the candle.

The High Priestess says: '*Guardians of the element of Earth, we summon, stir and call you to attend this rite and guard our Circle with the power and energy of the sacred standing stone.*'

She then draws an invoking pentagram of Earth (Figure 61) in front of the candle, visualising and feeling the Earth elementals arriving whilst the High Priest lights the candle with the taper. The High Priestess raises her athame in salute again. The High Priestess now continues drawing the line back to the northern candle to complete the circuit.

The High Priest takes his athame and casts a further Circle just inside the outer and on the inside of the candles marking the elements. He then returns to stand in front of the God candle. The Celestial Pentacle (Figure 62) is now fully formed. The space between the outer circle and inner circle can be used to place symbols relating to the turning of the wheel during a sabbat ceremony, or anything else (such as crystals) when raising energy, etc.

The High Priestess says: '*Lord and Lady, Goddess and God, we stand within this Circle of Power with the mighty ones duly called forth with our feet between the worlds of form and spirit. You bless us with your presence.*'

The High Priest pours the wine into the chalice and places the chalice in the hands of the High Priestess between her breasts (in front of her heart energy centre). She wills energy up from below her feet, through her base centre up to her heart centre and into the wine as the High Priest holds his athame in front of his heart and wills energy from above, though his crown, down to his heart centre and into the

▲ *Figure 62 – The Celestial Pentacle*

athame. As they continue to do this, the High Priest moves close to the High Priestess and lowers his athame into the wine saying: '*Man is to woman as God is to Goddess. I bless and consecrate this wine with the divine creative energy that brings life to all we undertake.*'

He places his athame on the altar. The High Priestess pours a libation into the water (or onto the earth if outside). She then hands the chalice to the High Priest who offers her the wine to drink whilst he holds the chalice. She takes the chalice and offers it to the Priest (note that each person should take a hearty mouthful rather than just a sip). The High Priestess then takes the wine around to any other Priests or Priestesses in the Circle (ideally working from one sex to the other in turn). When everyone has been blessed with the wine, the High Priestess finished any wine that remains.

The High Priestess then picks up the consecrating oil and draws a solar cross on the forehead of the High Priest. This is drawn in a particular way. The High Priestess says: '*I consecrate you in the name of the Goddess . . .*', she draws the horizontal line, '*and the God . . .*', she draws the vertical line, '*in this their Circle . . .*', she draws the circle around the solar cross (Figure 63).

The High Priest then takes the oil and draws the solar cross in the same way on the High Priestess, then consecrates everyone else in the Circle.

At this point any work or ritual that has been agreed beforehand is undertaken or performed. If it is an esbat ceremony then it would

▲ *Figure 63 – The Solar Cross*

normally start with the drawing down of the moon and the Charge of the Great Goddess, followed by healing, or any other magic that is deemed necessary either for those within the Circle or for those outside who have asked for help. If it is a sabbat ceremony then an appropriate ritual can be devised according to the time of year. However, the Circle can be cast at any time work is required and any time the cycle is appropriate for the type of work you intend to undertake.

When the work has been completed...

The High Priestess draws an invoking pentacle (Figure 64) of earth over the cakes or biscuits saying: '*I consecrate thee with the power of earth. May you bless and ground us at the end of our work.*'

The High Priestess ensures everyone has some of the cake (or a biscuit) and that a portion remains. (This portion is left outside after the ceremony has finished as an offering.)

The High Priestess and the High Priest then return to their positions in front of the north. The High Priest takes his athame in his receiving hand and picks up the circle he cast on the inner side of the perimeter walking from north in a widdershins direction. Once he has been

▲ *Figure 64 – Invoking pentagram of Earth*

185

around the circle he holds his athame, point up, to his forehead and visualises the energy returning into his body. The High Priestess then raises her athame and picks up the line drawn from north to Earth with the High Priest following to stand on her right.

The High Priestess says: '*Guardians of the element of Earth, we thank you for attending this rite and guarding our Circle, and ask for your blessings as you depart . . . hail and farewell.*'

The High Priestess draws a banishing pentagram of Earth (a reversal of the invoking pentagram) in front of the candle as the High Priest snuffs out the flame. All in the Circle say: '*Hail and farewell!*'

The High Priestess and High Priest bow their heads a little and then move to the Water candle in the same fashion.

The High Priestess says: '*Guardians of the element of Water, we thank you for attending this rite and guarding our Circle, and ask for your blessings as you depart . . . hail and farewell.*'

The High Priestess draws a banishing pentagram of Water in front of the candle as the High Priest snuffs out the flame. All in the Circle say: '*Hail and farewell!*'

The High Priestess and High Priest bow their heads a little. The High Priest now continues picking up the line from Water to Air as the High Priestess follows to stand on his left.

The High Priest says: '*Guardians of the element of Air, we thank you for attending this rite and guarding our Circle, and ask for your blessings as you depart . . . hail and farewell.*'

The High Priest draws a banishing pentagram of Air in front of the candle as the High Priestess snuffs out the flame. All in the Circle say: '*Hail and farewell!*'

The High Priestess and High Priest bow their heads a little and then move to the Fire candle in the same fashion.

The High Priest says: '*Guardians of the element of Fire, we thank you for attending this rite and guarding our Circle, and ask for your blessings as you depart . . . hail and farewell.*'

The High Priest draws a banishing pentagram of Fire in front of the candle as the High Priestess snuffs out the flame. All in the Circle say: '*Hail and farewell!*'

The High Priest continues to pick up the line to the north candle. The High Priestess follows to stand on his left. She picks up the candle and turns to face the centre of the Circle. The High Priest moves to stand in front of her with any others in the Circle. The High Priestess says: '*Love is the Law and Love is the bond. Merry did we meet and merry shall we meet again. Be blessed!*'

All respond: '*Blessed be!*'

High Priestess says: '*Lord and Lady, Goddess and God, you have blessed us with your presence. You are in our hearts always, so it must be.*'

The High Priest snuffs out the candle. The High Priestess then takes up her athame and picks up the outer Circle cast at the beginning, saying: '*The Circle is opened yet the Circle remains as the power is drawn back into me.*'

When she gets to the north she holds the athame, point up, to her forehead and allows the energy to be drawn back into her body. She then turns and everyone in the Circle put their arms around each other to hug and ground themselves.

Everything should be packed away neatly and with respect. Athames should be cleansed and protected with a little consecration oil.

13

HEALING – AN INTRODUCTION

There are literally hundreds of different forms of healing, many of them highly effective. Most Wiccans will incorporate several of these methods into their work at some stage as part of their calling, many end up specialising as healers. It is a skill for which there is certainly no shortage of clients.

There are a number of ethical considerations that Wiccans should explore before any form of healing is undertaken. In Wicca it is considered unethical to manipulate others against their will. Remember, this is the will of the Higher Self and not just that of the lower which may, or may not, be in tune with each other. Under no circumstances should healing be undertaken on somebody who has not asked for help or given permission, this would be interfering with their will. It should be considered, from the stance of a mentally and spiritually focused Wiccan, whether healing in all cases of illness or dysfunction is always the right course of action. There are many circumstances where lessons need to be learned by the person who is suffering that by interfering you may have blocked and therefore denied that person the opportunity to learn and grow. Issues related to stress and depression often fall into this category. Whilst you may well have developed skills of healing able to lift these symptoms without any effort on the part of the person suffering from them, would this necessarily be in the best interests of that person? It may be that they need to work things out for themselves and by doing so emerge a better balanced person for it. Would you want to deny them that opportunity? For this reason, developing a certain level of emotional detachment is of considerable value to anyone undertaking serious healing.

The method of healing needs to suit the circumstances. If the root cause is mental, as it often is with a stress related illness, then the treatment needs to applied on the mental level which may well require the skills of a counsellor more than that of someone channelling healing merely towards the physical symptoms, though in many cases the appropriate course of treatment is one that incorporates a number of complementary techniques rather than a single form. Drugs and surgery have their place though the medical profession often is very blinkered to the view that these are the only options open to them, which is most unfortunate. By all means work at developing and practising your healing skills, what-ever methods you seem drawn to, but never deny the person requiring healing the advice and opportunity of seeking professional help when circumstances are clearly of an acute nature.

If you undertake healing you will often gain remarkable results. Remember that healing is given with perfect love and perfect trust and that, no matter how good you appear to be at it, the success should not go to your head. Thank the Goddess and God for enabling you to channel the healing to where it is needed and don't let your successes inflate your ego, which will only work towards creating imbalances that are unhelpful to both you and those you intend to help.

COLOUR HEALING

Colour has a powerful and complementary effect on attitudes generally and can be applied to good effect when healing oneself or working with those around you. Colour, whether it be of the room or of the clothes, can have a profound effect on the emotional level where many illnesses and imbalances can go on to cause physical symptoms. The colours need to be appropriate to the needs.

Purple is generally a good all-round healing colour being associated with the spiritual plane and a mixture of calming blue and red for strength. Blues can be very calming for the mental level and help to create a cooling and calming atmosphere. Green is a terrific healing colour, often incorporated in distance healing, as it is associated with the heart centre from where healing energy is often channelled. Yellow can be very useful for raising the spirit being the colour associated with the Sun and being bright and cheerful. Orange, associated with the sacral centre, is highly creative and active and reds are great for bringing the deeper fiery strength needed to fight off many of the physical ailments. Pink can be a very calming peaceful colour. Brown is a very sickly colour and is best avoided during any healing work.

Black and white are closely related and represent the dual energies of Goddess and God. Both black and white work with all the colours of the rainbow. If you take a prism you are able to separate the seven rainbow colours from white light. If you take pigments representing those same colours and mix them together you will create black. Black is receptive, associated with matter, and absorbs light energy. White is radiant and reflects light energy. Those who wear black will find that they draw energy towards them more readily (which can be quite draining for those around them in quite a vampiric way) and those who wear white tend to exude greater confidence and radiate energy out.

HEALING WITH THE HANDS

Healing by channelling energy through the hands is one of the easiest and most readily available methods. It is sometimes known as Reiki, though that is a form that has its roots in the Japanese culture and incorporates all sorts of symbols completely alien to the western mind. However, the energy channelled through Reiki is exactly the same as any other healing energy being channelled. There is only one divine source even though it may go under numerous different names from one culture to the next. A High Priestess I work with also happens to be a Reiki Master and has worked in a number of different Reiki traditions. Having demonstrated my own methods, with only little knowledge of Reiki symbolism, she kindly admitted that my methods were much the same and just as effective.

I have found that healing in this way requires a strong connection with the Goddess and God. For this reason the amount of work a witch does on a daily basis in building up, developing and maintaining this relationship is synonymous with the degree to which the healing is effective.

Figure 65 shows the position of the seven major energy centres (or chakra centres) that most people working in the esoteric field are familiar with. These centres, located in the etheric part of the physical body, act as receptors and transmitters working with the seven ray energies that link the physical with the other planes. The figure also shows the location of the lesser energy centres. Notice that the lesser energy centres include one in the centre of each palm. It is these energy centres that we use as the interface between the energies flowing through us into the person we are working with.

The witch first of all ensures that person being treated is relaxed, has understood what you are doing, and why. Ensure you have their full understanding and permission. Without this there will inevitably be etheric blockages that will render the healing ineffectual. This trust and faith in you and the technique does not imply that faith is the method

✖️ **MAJOR**
✶ **LESSER**

▲ *Figure 65 – Major and Lesser Energy (or 'Chakra') Centres*

of healing, merely that a level of faith is required in order to accept the flow of energy. Once the person is relaxed, ensure they are comfortable, either sitting in a chair or laying down. It is important that you are able to move around them without causing yourself discomfort. Next, call openly, or mentally, on the Goddess and God for assistance in healing this person and strengthen the connection by visualising the energy flowing through you from the base centre and the crown, merging at the heart, them flowing down your arms to your palms. You should feel this energy flowing mentally and physically. Remember that the energy is not coming *from* you, but flowing *through* you. If you give your own energy you will only drain yourself, which is not the aim of this process. To enable the energy to flow into the person's energy field, gently hold your palms, face down, either side of their shoulders, level with their throat energy centre. It is not usually necessary to focus in on the area needing healing (or rather the area you *think* needs

191

healing as it may well actually be elsewhere), just trust that the healing energy will find its way to where it is needed.

At the end of this process ensure that both you and your patient are both thoroughly grounded. The energy flow often leaves one or both of you feeling quite light-headed. A short and sharp flick of the fingers is sometimes useful to help the grounding process, to get rid of any negative energy that may have entered your own etheric field, and to ensure the flow of energy has ceased. Nothing more elaborate is necessary in most circumstances.

DISTANCE HEALING

Healing can be very effective over distance. Energy can be transferred easily from one place to another on the higher planes because time and space do not operate in those planes in the way we experience them on the physical. Your ability to heal over distance will be greatly enhanced, once again, by the ability to visualise, which is yet another reason why it is important to maintain the discipline of meditation.

It is generally considered unethical to offer healing to anyone unless they have asked for it or accepted your offer of healing. To do otherwise would be considered manipulative and you may be throwing healing towards someone who has important lessons to learn through the disease. If you are doing healing over a distance, obtaining a picture of the person, or some personal effect, will greatly aid the work. I often utilise my altar for such work. Once the energy has been sent through a visualisation I usually put the candle I have been using during the work on my altar, on top of or next to any photo, so that the candle can burn out and continue to take the energy to where it is intended. I will surround this candle and the photo with crystals or herbs that I consider will aid the healing. The altar is a sacred space entirely suitable for this sort of work.

If you are certain of the type of energy that is going to be a most benefit to the recipient then you can use a candle of an appropriate colour. If the nature of the disease is not clear then using a general purpose green candle will help to send the energy to that person's heart energy centre where it can dissipate to where ever it is needed the most. Once you have chosen a candle, consecrate it with some healing oil such as lavender (which is good in most cases) and spend a short while with the candle in your hands focusing on the person intended. This is where a photo will come in most useful. Once you have done this then put the candle in a stand and light it from your central altar candle and close your eyes to meditate. Offer your blessings to the Lady and Lord and ask for their help in your work. If you feel it is appropriate you can also call on your guides to help you if they are willing. Next, visualise as strongly as you can, the person surrounded by a brilliant white light. Hold the vision for as long as you can, as clearly as you can, then let the energy settle. Remember to thank the spirits that may have helped you, thank the Goddess and God, then leave the candle burning at the altar.

If you are going to leave the candle unattended be very careful how it is left. It is not a good idea to leave a candle burning if you are going to leave the home unless you have perhaps put it, on its own, inside something like an aluminium basin where it can do no harm whatever happens to it.

If you are able to offer healing of this sort as a coven or a group then the extra energy offered will help the process enormously. Covens often maintain healing lists for people who have asked for help and channel energy in their direction at every opportunity.

HEALING VISUALISATION

The visualisation that follows is written for use in a group and can be read out by any member. It is best done in a fully cast Circle, though this is not entirely necessary. There have been times when I have used this one, being a thoroughly modern witch, with a group meeting in an Internet chat room, and to good effect. The person reading it out should do so slowly with plenty of breaks to allow for the visualisation to develop.

This is a visualisation aimed at sending healing energy out to wherever it is needed in the world. It can easily be adapted to send healing to an individual if required.

Make sure you are comfortable ... As you slow your breathing you are perfectly calm and relaxed ...

We are standing in an ancient stone circle, facing each other. There is soft fine grass between us, lichen growing on the old silver-grey stones ... There is the sweet scent of lavender in the air ... Invite your friendly spirit guides and helpers to join us if they wish ... As we breathe gently, we notice the air is fresh and clear ... As we breathe in, we breathe clear cleansing light, purifying our body, clearing our mind. As we breathe out we let any dark impurity expel itself from our body ... Around our circle there is a mysterious gentle mist. We hear the birds cheerfully chirping ... we hear rabbits running around playfully. This is a peaceful place ... The grass sparkles with little diamonds of dew. Feel the grass between your toes ... Open the soles of your feet to the earth and begin to feel the energy rise up in you . . . Feel your connection with the earth . . . Draw from deep down like the roots of a great oak tree . . . As the energy builds up in you, open your crown chakra to the abundant Universal energy from above . . . The golden Universal light floods into your crown, mixing with the earth energies . . . allow it to flow out of your heart chakra into the middle of our circle . . . A bright glow builds up in the circle and begins to get brighter and brighter . . . It is now so bright and powerful that it extends beyond us, beyond our circle . . . As we keep the energy flowing, the light dissolves the mist and sweeps across green valleys and hills . . . The healing light sweeps across rivers and seas to everyone who has asked for help . . . See those people surrounded by our golden healing light bringing peace and calm to their lives . . . see them smile . . . As we draw yet more energy, the light continues to sweep across the planet, bringing peace and harmony to every place it reaches . . . The healing energy helps those involved in conflict find peaceful solutions, it brings an end to pain and sorrow in the world and eases the suffering of all life – plant and animal . . . As the energy continues to grow and the light intensifies further we move out to the stars above and look back at our home floating through space like a bright jewel in the Universe . . . See the planet glow, like a bright star . . . surrounded by a golden halo . . . Keep the energy flowing . . . see the bright glow and feel the love and pure joy embrace our Earth . . . Now, when you are ready, gently let the light begin to subside . . . See the energy settle where it is most needed . . . In your own time, come back to our circle . . . Feel your gentle, deep breathing again . . . Send any remaining energy back down the roots to the earth, saving enough for your own needs . . . It is a bright summer day . . . feel the beautifully fresh air fill your lungs . . . Thank your guides and helpers. Let them know they are free to stay or leave . . . Seal your aura. You are a creature of beauty and light . . .

Blessings be to one and all.

14

SEX MAGIC

The issue of sex is one that many people shy away from. This is a great shame as it is, in its way, what lays at the heart of creation. It is the sexual relationship, metaphysically speaking, between Goddess and God – two opposite but complementing energies – that create everything from the cosmic to the microcosmic.

Amongst the first advanced pagan communities of the world, in Crete and Egypt for instance, the creative cosmic forces were seen as the relationship between goddesses and gods. Similar energies and relationships were seen between other aspects of the Goddess and God all around them – in the seas, rivers and fields, in the mountains, the valleys, the woods and the plains. Everywhere they looked they saw the complementary energies of male and female merging to create and to provide. They did not think of this sexual relationship as something dirty or something to be ashamed of; far from it: it was at the heart of Nature and everything around them from the biggest things to the smallest. For thousands of years they followed the natural ways and lived, as men and women, emulating the rest of nature and the harmony that is inherent in such a balance. Neither sex dominated the other. Each had their roles and they undertook these roles as nature intended. The act of sex was one that was a celebration of life and created life. It was celebrated in their work which included art depicting the sexual act as something open, natural and sacred.

It wasn't until relatively modern times, when the Age of Pisces approached, that one sex began to exert dominion over the other and created an imbalance. The Hebrew text explaining creation was written around 500 BCE as the book of Genesis. For the first time in a somewhat twisted parody of the earlier pagan creation myths, the female form, representing the Goddess, was blamed for thrusting humans into shame. The concept that clothing was essential to cover this shame was first introduced. Several hundred years later St Paul, a Hebrew born in pagan Greece under the rulership of the Romans, spread the message that sex was shameful and that the naked form was equally shameful. This concept has survived in Christianity and the whole concept has survived the entire Age of Pisces. Women have been held back and denigrated by men who fear their power through an age dominated by war, disharmony and imbalance. It is not surprising that now, as we approach a new age, that many women feel angry about this. Even within some Wiccan circles, Dianic Wicca for instance, the feminine element dominates the male (if indeed the masculine exists at all). This is a sign that the pendulum is swinging back the other way, understandably, but as pagans we need to remember that it is the balance between Goddess and God that brings the creative energy and harmony that we need.

The human body, contrary to years of male-dominated religion, is not something to be ashamed of. The act of sex is not 'sinful' but a natural and joyful and one that emulates the Goddess and God and everything they provide in nature. Accepting that the act of sex is something to be celebrated does not mean to say that we should live promiscuously or partake in the sort of raging orgies that those of other paths would like to imagine. The relationship between man and woman is a natural one, one that potentially offers the fulfilment of our creative possibilities. Being able to talk about sex openly and honestly is a sign of maturity, a sign that we have grown beyond the centuries of sexual repression and control, not a sign that we are shedding our responsibilities or becoming weak – quite the reverse.

Wiccan is a relatively new revival of the pagan ways that is gaining a great deal of popularity. Unfortunately we are inevitably going through a phase where this openness towards sex is going to be misconstrued by the millions of people who have suffered sexual repression not just through this life, but through several previous ones too. It has to be said that some people, usually men, are attracted to the Craft because they want to express this sexual freedom in ways that can be quite abusive. This needs to be guarded against. Working skyclad with others, when it happens, needs to work above the lower emotional level. It allows us to celebrate our bodies and loosen our inhibitions as well as to allow energy to flow unfettered. It is not about being sexually promiscuous but about being uninhibited, about working with the Goddess and God and their energies openly with perfect love and perfect trust. Having said all that, however, it is worth pointing out that working naked is far from absolutely necessary. The call to 'go naked to your rites' is often taken literally whereas it would be more appropriate to interpret it as being naked on a spiritual level, that is – leaving the ego behind and being totally open with the Goddess and God without any preconceptions. It is only through being totally open that we can received the full benefit of what they have to offer us and they can receive the best of what we can offer them in return.

The bond between those who have entered a partnership, whether it is legally recognised as a marriage or not, is a sacred one. It personifies the sacred marriage between Goddess and God and is essentially a contract to conduct their work on the physical plane. The bond should be on a mental and spiritual level, not just an emotional one. Nothing should be able to break this bond if it is properly on the higher levels. Even if working naked in a Circle with others, even if some degree of sexual energy is raised, this does not need to challenge the relationship between bonded partners in any way as long as they are able to trust one another. If the bond at the mental and spiritual levels is strong then nothing can come between that trust. Unfortunately far too many part-nerships are purely emotional, or worse, driven by the expectations of the society in which they are trapped, and the sacredness of such a partnership is never experienced.

SEXUAL ENERGIES

Earlier in this book we have given some consideration to the seven main energy centres. The nature of these energy centres, that bring energy into the physical body from all the planes, is that they are active. The energy at each point rotates in a direction opposite to that of the points either side of it enabling the energy raised from above or below to spiral through the body in a serpent like fashion. One of the differences between women and men is that the way in which each of their energy centres rotates is opposite that of the other sex – they do, after all represent the Goddess and God, the two polarities. This is symbolised by the caduceus. When a woman and man face each other, as in the more basic sexual posi-tions, their energy centres are therefore complementing each other and potentially working together. They are able to raise energies together in a way that it would be impossible for those of a similar sex to ever achieve (even if they were to facing the same direction to get the energy centres flowing together – the polarities would not allow full and proper combina-tion). This, therefore, gives us a clue as to how a woman and man working together can raise powerful and balanced energies from all the planes.

The normal position for two witches (male a female) to make love whilst raising energy to put into a magical act is as follows. The man sits on the floor with legs crossed so that his root energy centre is on the ground and most readily able to raise Earth energies into his body. The woman then sits astride the man with her legs wrapped around his body and ensures the man's penis is directed into her vagina. The woman, as the Goddess, takes control of the motion. Both participants need to focus on the energies being raised from the Earth and spiralling up through their bodies around the energy centres in a serpent-like fashion. This needs to done slowly at first and each of the partners feeling the energy rise up simultaneously. When the energy has been raised through each body to the crown it is then sent down through their partner's body, again going around the energy centres. When it reaches the base again, it transfers back to the other person with further energy raised from the Earth. This continues circulating around and around. Gradually the energy raised grows enormous potential and gets to the point where it is no longer circulating from one to another but is merging into one. The woman generally needs to judge when this has happened – it can be readily felt. When as much energy has been raised that the woman feels unable to hold on to any more, she releases it through her crown and sends it to add an enormous jolt of energy to whatever spell had been the purpose. Both should visualise giving birth to this work. For this to work most effectively, it is best for both to reach the point of orgasm together, but even if the man reaches that point first, the energy is released when the woman reaches orgasm; it is the Goddess who gives birth to any act of creation.

Sex, or the act of making love, is only an exoteric (though powerful and effective) way of raising energy. It should be emphasised that the act of sex is not the energy that is raised, but it stimulates the energy centres in an appropriate way, though this can be done without undergoing the sexual act itself. What you are doing is drawing energy from the Earth, forcing it through the sacral centre with your will, through the other centres and out through the crown. The sexual act enables you to do this without a great deal of conscious control, but it is not the only way.

One way of readily recalling the force of raising the energy in this way is by psychologically introducing an associated symbol whilst making love. At the point of climax, whilst making love with your partner, or even whilst masturbating, you touch your forefinger against your crown, or even something more subtle like touching your thumb to your ring finger, you will at a later date be able to raise the energies in a similar way simply by association. This is a useful skill as you are able to use this without drawing attention to yourself if out in a crowd when need arises.

Energies can be raised in a group or alone using the energy flowing through the centres without the sexual act. Having sex in a group is potentially powerful, but the level of trust required for this to work successfully without serious repercussions afterward are rare and should be avoided like the plague unless that trust is based on a long-term and close friendship. I would point out here that some groups have allowed this sexual activity to get out of hand and allowed themselves to be diverted down a dark and dead-end path. This is a sacred rite, not a lustful orgy!

RAISING ENERGY WITHOUT SEX

'Sexual energy' can be raised in a group situation using the same energy centres without performing the sexual act.

If working in a group it is useful to have an equal number of women and men, though this ideal can be difficult to achieve. The energies are raised slowly, as in the act of love making, and built up to a crescendo where the energy is released to form the 'cone of power' from the group to put a similar jolt of energy into a spell. A good way of achieving this is to incorporate both chanting and dance/movement.

A priestess (ideally a high priestess) lies on the floor in the centre of a fully cast Circle with her head to the north. She will need her athame or a wand. The rest of the group needs to be of even numbers, ideally equal numbers of men and women, though this isn't essential if an ideal is not possible. They stand equally spaced around the priestess lying on the floor. A number of three-foot long red, white and black cords are used – one for each couple. (White, red and black symbolise the triple aspects of the Goddess – maiden, mother and crone – or to the process of rebirth, life and death.) One end of each cord is held by the partner standing directly opposite; where the cords cross in the middle they are looped together. Where they cross should be approximately above the womb of the priestess lying on the floor who holds her athame or wand pointing up with its base on her womb.

When all is set, the priestess on the floor begins to visualise the manifested work in hand. The others begin to walk in unison slowly around in a deosil direction and begin to chant at the same pace they are walking. There is no need to use a complicated chant, it is better to be short, concise and rhythmic. One of those chanting, agreed beforehand, needs to take the lead and set the pace. Gradually the chanting begins to pick up pace and get faster and faster. At the same time the movement gets faster and faster in line with the chanting. When the chanting can not get any faster and enough energy is buzzing around the Circle, the priestess on the floor shouts: '3 ... 2 ... 1 ...' and where zero would have been the cords are released with a scream, thrown up into the air, as the priestess on the floor thrusts her athame or wand upwards in the same direction and brings the focus on the work manifesting, as do all the others as they collapse on the floor.

It is a good idea to follow this with the ceremony of cakes and wine to ensure everyone is thoroughly grounded.

SOLITARY RITUAL

The following ritual is one that I have inherited from a long-standing Alexandrian High Priest with a few minor adaptations of my own. It is a solitary ritual that invokes the power of the horned God into one's body to strengthen and enliven the inner flame. It is designed to be carried out at Candlemass, otherwise known as Imbolg, as the Sun is returning to warm our land and our hearts at the first stirrings of spring. It is intended to symbolically raise energy through oneself in order to ensure the fertility of the land, though it equally helps to raise the energy within in preparation for a creatively fertile season. Many pagans today celebrate the festival of Imbolg, or Candlemass, on the 1st or 2nd of February. To me, as I feel the modern calendar is completely off sync, I would more likely choose the date of the first full Moon after the Sun moves into Aquarius (which it does late in January). This would most likely fall around the same time, but would be more in tune with appropriate energy flows between the Sun and Moon.

As this is a solitary ritual, there are two versions of the words shown here. One for priests, the other for priestesses. It obviously needs to be done in private and alone. It is best performed naked, though I would suggest that if you are in the UK and are able to do this outside, then being naked will most likely result in hypothermia! In such situations either do it outdoors with plenty of warm clothes on, or inside, preferably where you can see the Moon. The ritual is best performed at midnight.

You will need four candles set at the quarters marking Earth, Air, Fire and Water. You do not require an altar – you are the altar effectively. You will also need a small cauldron or a thick solid brass bowl. You also need something completely heatproof to stand this on as it will get *very* hot. Methylated spirits are poured into the cauldron so that it is around half full. You are going to set light to the meths, so you need to be very, very careful as if it spills you will have a major fire on your hands! The only other things you will need within the Circle are you athame and a lighting taper.

Place the cauldron (or brass bowl) in a position so that when you are sitting in the centre of the Circle, the cauldron is between you and the Moon towards which you will be facing. Ensure that you have poured an appropriate amount of meths into the cauldron and that it is well away from anything that can catch fire and is on something very heat-proof. Remember – this is going to get very hot and it will be a while before you can safely pick the cauldron up afterwards. Using your athame, cast the Circle and call the quarters in the normal way, then move to sit facing the Moon in front of the cauldron and meditate quietly for a few moments. When you are ready, stand, take the taper and light it from the candle marking Fire, then set light to the methylated spirits – it should burn with a gorgeous tall purple and yellow flame. Extinguish the taper and move to stand in front of the flame with your legs parted and arms raised in the pentagram or Goddess position. Next use one of the following verses (as appropriate to your sex).

Priests:

> *Ancient of ancients,*
> *Rayed in beauty,*
> *Horny with power,*
> *Hurry to me.*
> *Without thy light and warmth,*
> *I shall surely die.*
> *Tis Candlemass and I await thee.*
> *Warm the sleeping seed within the belly,*
> *Of our Earth Mother.*
> *Quicken and comfort me,*
> *Renew my strength.*
> *Look, I have kindled a fire of welcome,*
> *My fire burns brightly.*
> *Sustain my horn of power,*
> *In a mighty erection.*
> *I do faithfully serve thee.*
> *Hasten and warm,*
> *My cold and frozen land.*
> *I bid thee welcome.*

Priestesses:

> *Ancient of ancients,*
> *Rayed in beauty,*
> *Horny with power,*
> *Hurry to me.*

Without thy light and warmth,
I shall surely die.
Tis Candlemass and I await thee.
Warm the sleeping seed within the belly,
Of our Earth Mother.
Quicken and comfort me,
Renew my strength.
Look, I have kindled a fire of welcome,
My fire burns brightly,
Sustain my fiery Cauldron,
Upon thy horn of Power.
Seduce me with Thy might erection.
I am Thine and Thou art mine.
Hasten to me,
Keep me unto Thyself.
Love me as no other can,
For I am Thine alone.

You can then sit down and meditate with the flame. Allow yourself to become one with the flame and feel the energy rising through your body, enlivening your energy centres. As the actual flame dies down, visualise the flame continuing to burn inside you for as long as you can. Ideally this would be done until sunrise, but that does take a great deal of discipline. If any thoughts about your activities planned for the coming season come into your mind as visualisations, make a mental note of these as soon as possible after the ritual. These are the seeds of things coming to fruition later in the year.

Finally – another reminder that even after the flame has died down, the cauldron will remain very hot for some time. Allow it to cool down thoroughly before you attempt to move it. The flame will have thoroughly cleansed the cauldron for further use. It is therefore prepared, once cooled, for you to place any talismans, amulets or seals inside that are symbolic of the activities you intend to work on in the months of fertility ahead.

THE GREAT RITE

The Great Rite is essentially a symbolic representation of the sexual union between Goddess and God. As such it can take one of two forms in a ritual. Either a symbolic rite utilising the chalice and the athame, or it can be performed in actuality if in private and your partner is your normal sexual partner and used to working with you. Whether it be symbolic or actual, the Great Rite clearly requires two, one of each gender . . .

Priest and Priestess move to centre of circle, she with her back to the altar, and he with his back to the South.

Priestess lays herself on the ground, hips in centre of circle, head to altar, arms and legs outstretched to form the pentacle.

Priest fetches a veil and lays it over her, covering from breasts to knees. He kneels facing her with his knees at her feet. He takes out his athame and takes hold of the chalice.

Priest delivers the invocation . . .

'Goddess of the Stars and of the Earth,
In your womb all things grow,
And from your womb all things enter life,
And to you all things return.
We are of you, as you are of us.
This Woman before me is your Priestess,
An Earthly representation of you,
And we place her womb in the centre of our Circle,
As our great altar before which we worship.
This is as things should be,
In honour of you our Goddess who we love and adore.
That which we love and adore we also invoke.
Queen of the Stars, Mother of all, Jewel of light,
Who transcends all time and space,
By seed and root, and stem and bud,
Leaf and flower and fruit, we invoke you,
Into this your Priestess.'

Priest removes the veil.

Priest continues . . .

'Altar of mysteries manifest,
The sacred Circle's secret point.
I sign you as of old,
With my lips anoint you.'

The Priest than kisses the Priestess on her right foot, womb, left foot, right knee, left knee, right foot and finally on her womb. This represents the active pentagram of the spirit.

If the Rite is symbolic then the Priestess kneels and takes the chalice from the High Priest and the High Priest lowers the point of his athame into the wine. Both use both hands for this. If the Rite is actual then the Priest lays on top of the Priestess guiding his phallus into her vagina.

Priest continues:

'Here where the lance and grail unite,
Where the Goddess meets the God,
Uniting as One within you,
Do we understand the Great Mystery.'

Priest puts his athame on the altar then places both hands around the chalice. He kisses her, she sips the wine; she kisses him, he sips the wine. The chalice is then replaced on the altar.

A NOTE OF CHANTS

Chanting plays an important function in ritual work. It can be used to help focus the intended energies as well as helping to raise 'the Cone of Power' working the energies up from the base centre to the crown.

Some chants have been used in this volume and others can be found throughout the many versions of the Book of Shadows found in other books and throughout the wide world of the Internet. It should be remembered that it is always better to devise your own chants for a specific purpose rather than to use one devised by someone else for a different purpose. The process of creating a chant is part of the creative process and thus part of your work.

In Wicca you may at times come across a traditional chant or pagan salute in the form of 'IO EVOHE'. I would like to end this volume with a note on this and its origins in a effort to leave you with some final thoughts on Wicca's connection with other paths and to bring this volume full circle so to speak. This chant or salute, it seems, was brought into Wicca originally by Gerald Gardner. In 1953, Gardner wrote: *'Of old there were many chants and songs used especially in dances. Many of these have been forgotten by us here, but we know that they used cries of IAU which seems muchly like the cries of EVO or EVOHE of the ancients. Much dependeth on the pronunciation if this be so. In my youth, when I heard IAU it seemed to be AEIOU, or rather, AAAEEIOOOOUU. This may be but the natural way to prolong it to make it fit for a call, but it suggests that these be possibly the initials of an invocation as Agla is said to be, and of sooth 'tis said that the whole Hebrew alphabet is said to be such, and for this reason is recited as a most powerful charm, but at least this is certain, these cries during the dances do have profound effect, as I myself have seen ...'*

It should be pointed out here that it is extreme folly to use words that one does not understand. This important rule applies to words in an unfamiliar foreign language, as well as words you assume have no meaning. At best the exercise would be pointless and meaningless, at worst you maybe invoking energies that you don't appreciate.

What I believe Gardner was referring to here is a sacred and ancient chant with deep esoteric meaning with connections to the seven planes that help to invoke the energies through those planes from physical to spiritual and back. The correct form is 'OEAOHOO'. Oeaohoo represents the root form of the 'Father-Mother of the Gods' in the Stanzas of Dyzan, as extrapolated by Helena Blavatsky in the Secret Doctrine. Each of the seven letters represents one of the seven planes and the resulting word, phrase or chant can be expressed in a number of ways, which may explain Gardner's uncertainty about the way he claims to have heard it. Each letter can be pronounced individually if done slowly, but then as the chant becomes faster the syllables gradually blend together, first into five, then four, then three and finally one melding, symbolically, the planes together and bringing the energies of the Goddess and God together as one.

Until volume 2, merry part and blessed be!